I'll Stay as Long as I can

Written by
Claire Emily Nelson
and
Margery Clara Nelson

Edited by
Ann Fisher

iUniverse, Inc.
New York   Bloomington

I'll Stay as Long as I Can
Mother and Daughter Diaries of Love, Tragedy and Remembrance

Copyright © 2008 by Margery Nelson

All rights reserved. No part of this book may be used or reproduced by any means, graphic, electronic, or mechanical, including photocopying, recording, taping or by any information storage retrieval system without the written permission of the publisher except in the case of brief quotations embodied in critical articles and reviews.

The views expressed in this work are solely those of the author and do not necessarily reflect the views of the publisher, and the publisher hereby disclaims any responsibility for them.
iUniverse books may be ordered through booksellers or by contacting:

iUniverse
1663 Liberty Drive
Bloomington, IN 47403
www.iuniverse.com
1-800-Authors (1-800-288-4677)

Because of the dynamic nature of the Internet, any Web addresses or links contained in this book may have changed since publication and may no longer be valid. The views expressed in this work are solely those of the author and do not necessarily reflect the views of the publisher, and the publisher hereby disclaims any responsibility for them.

ISBN: 978-0-595-51071-9 (pbk)
ISBN: 978-0-595-61755-5 (ebk)

Printed in the United States of America

iUniverse Rev. Date 11/4/08

Dedication

This book is dedicated to my three wonderful children:

Claire Emily, my youngest child. Her determination and willingness to put a smile on a horrible battle were an inspiration to us all. Claire's diaries remind us of what a delight she was and how much we miss her.

Hayley Anne, my beautiful middle child. She has stood by me through everything. Her unrelenting support and love have encouraged me and given me the strength to go on.

Grant Clayton, my first child. When I had him, I learned what love really was. Raising him was an incredible challenge, yet it was worth every minute of it. I'm so proud of him and the person he is today.

Thank you, all three of you. You have made my journey on this earth incredibly worthwhile.

Acknowledgements

This book would not have been written without the loving help of my family and friends. I want to thank them in the order in which they got involved in the book.

Grant: when I came up with the idea of publishing Claire's diary, he was the first one to say "Go for it, Mom!"

My dear friend, Shelley, was the first to read Claire's Diary, and she suggested that I add my diaries to Claire's to complete the story.

Hayley was there the whole way, encouraging me, and helping me edit Claire's writing.

My sister, Cindy, took the rough manuscript, cleaned it up and placed it in the diary format.

From the start, Uncle Gordon and Aunty Lee have been beside me, encouraging me to get Claire's message out.

Ann Fisher is my wonderful editor. She made the many changes necessary to make it the book it is today.

Finally, my brother, Chuck, designed the present cover and helped me with the final editing and printing that have captured the essence of Claire.

Of course, there are many other people who have encouraged me along the way, and if I forgot anyone, I apologize. Thank you, everyone for helping us create a lasting memory of Claire.

Introduction

After my daughter, Claire, passed away from a brain tumor, I kept finding her diaries around the house. I finally counted them, and she had written in ten diaries over a ten year period. Slowly, afraid of what I might feel; I began to go through the diaries.

I found these wonderful stories of a girl who loved every minute of her life. It was like Claire was alive again, and speaking to me through her written words. I could hear her voice as I read, something I had longed to hear since the day she left this earth.

As I continued to transcribe her diaries, I began to realize that she had left them to me so that they would be published. She wanted to share her life with the world, before and after cancer.

Claire wants us to use her diaries to raise money to fight childhood cancer.

If we can prevent another family from going through what we did, Claire's death will not have been in vain.

Claire was a beautiful, bright, delightful person who faced life with joy, humor, faith and courage. She was loved by so many people, and though she was only with us for sixteen short years, we're grateful for the time we had with her, and the wonderful memories she has left us.

*Hayley, Grant, Mom + me
Five and Tinkerbell
August 1998*

June 1995 - Margy
    To Claire,
    My very special Fairy whom I love very much and always will. This is your very first diary, write what you feel.
Love,
Mommy

June 2, 1995 - Claire
    Today at school, it was field day and it was fun. My sister has gone camping and my mom and I had fun playing Samantha and cleaning my room. I can't wait to paint it!

Mommy and me with our American Girl dolls

June 4, 1995 - Claire

Today at lunch, Clay and Jake were playing around. So we did not get a blue star or get to go to sleep.

June 10, 1995 - Margy

My children are growing up way too fast! They are now on summer break from school and it is so much fun to have them home.

This is our first summer in our big new home. We moved from Tucker, GA to Alpharetta, GA. We chose Alpharetta because of the great school systems, especially with Grant's issues.

We love this neighborhood. That is, the kids and I love the neighborhood. Dave, my husband, doesn't. He says the neighbors are all "Pleasant Valley Sundays" that mow their lawns on Saturday" Whatever that means. It's kind of funny, though, because Dave was the one who picked out this house.

Anyway, back to the kids. We live in a swim and tennis neighborhood, the kids and I go to the pool every day.

Grant is my red haired boy and will turn ten on June 16. What a wonderful, enthusiastic person, so full of life, yet sensitive. Since finding out about his attention deficit disorder, we have adjusted and so has he. He's now much happier with himself (of course the ADHD and antidepressant medications help with that). Grant's dyslexia is a lot better, too. He never wanted to read until Dave bought him "Calvin and Hobbs" books. He was so fascinated by the story of Calvin, as told in pictures, (Dave used the read the cartoons in the paper to him) it motivated him to want to learn to read. Grant still doesn't read at grade level, but each year he is getting closer. He still doesn't have any friends, but I am hopeful he will soon. Luckily, he doesn't seem to miss them. He is a very visual person and an artist. I'm constantly amazed at the ideas Grant comes up with.

The only thing that worries me about my son is that his asthma has gotten worse. He was so sick this spring; he had to be on breathing treatments four times a day and steroids. He's better now that summer is here, but fall and spring are brutal on him. If this continues, we may have to rip up the carpeting in his room to see if that helps.

Hayley is a serene, hopeful, thoughtful and loving eight-year- old. She's very verbal and constantly working things out in her mind. She's very logical, precise, and her imagination reflects this. She'll make "fairy stew "with flowers one hour and work on the computer the next.

Claire (alias Tink because she loves Tinkerbell so much) is talkative, enthusiastic, active, fearless (taught herself to climb across the monkey bars at three years old) and just fun to be around. You never know what will pop out of her mouth. Last week it was "Mom, I need to ask you a strange question—will my breasts be as big as yours someday?" Then she'll be on to something else. She tells me twenty times a day "I love you" and wants to be with me all the time.

I continue to make and sculpt dolls and I am finally on the road (not there yet) to becoming a very good doll artist. I wrote two articles for doll magazines that were published! If I can keep going this way, maybe I'll never have to go back to nursing. Sometimes Dave will allude to the fact that I would make a lot more money as a nurse, instead of as a doll maker. (being a doctor, Dave would know this). Of course, he's one to talk. He doesn't like patient care and has chosen to be in research, so his opinion is skewed. I just ignore his comments, although, sometimes I feel like I never left nursing given all the problems Grant has had (ADHD, speech problems, dyslexia, asthma).

And finally, my marriage: continues to be a struggle, good days and bad. With Dave's depressions and the many moves, (all but one his choice) our marriage just feels like an ongoing struggle. I realize I don't even know what a healthy marriage is. I do know that Dave's inconsistency makes it hard to trust him emotionally, even though he seems less depressed right now.

I truly hope and pray we can work things out, but the power struggles are wearing me down.

April 9. 1997 - Claire

Today I visited my dad. We played football. Ate dinner and played twister. I wish that I could see a fairy. That is what I want to happen. Also, Hayley hurt my feelings. Good night for now! I will tell you what I do tomorrow. Good Night!

April 9, 1997 - Margy

The children are at Dave's for the weekend. Claire has already called twice, so I know that they are okay. When they are gone, I miss them so much and worry about them.

Dave and I have been separated for four months. It feels like four years. This has been the hardest thing ever in my life. We now talk only through our attorneys. I worry about paying the bills, but luckily the judge gave me a good temporary alimony. I just feel so scared all the time, and it's like we're living in limbo. Still, I know our breakup was inevitable. Now if we can just get through the pending divorce without too much animosity.

The one good thing is that the kids are doing better. Grant is doing so well, because Dave isn't around to constantly criticize and yell at him.

Grant is eleven years old, and in fifth grade. I hope our marriage counselor was right when he said that Grant would settle down when he reached his teens. He's at that age where they argue all the time about anything. School also continues to be a battle, even though he is in special education classes. He and I spend two to three hours a night on his homework.Luckily, his asthma lessened after we pulled up the carpeting last year.

He still has no friends, but doesn't seem to notice this. Wish I didn't. Sometimes, when he is building his Leggo towns or playing in the sandbox, it's like he's in his own little world.

Hayley is now nine years old. Her night terrors, that were so bad before the separation; have subsided, and she isn't afraid to go to school. In fact, she likes school again. When I first took her to the marriage counselor to find out about the night terrors, the counselor said Hayley was having them because Dave was yelling at Grant every night, and Hayley was afraid for her brother. Unfortunately I didn't realize this because I would tuck the children into bed and go down to the basement to work on my dolls. Dave would go back upstairs and yell at Grant because he was so slow getting ready for bed, or whatever. I wish I had realized what was going on.

It was pretty embarrassing for the three children to have to tell their friends about the separation.I enrolled them in Rainbows, a support group for children with parents going through a divorce, and that seems to be helping.

Claire is now seven years old and in second grade. After hating preschool because she had to leave me, she has turned out to LOVE grade school. She plans her clothes each day, studies very hard, and enjoys every day to the fullest. She still loves to be with me, probably more than the other two did at this age, but maybe the separation has affected that. Still, I'll miss it when she no longer thinks I hung the moon.

Last Wednesday, when we were waiting for Dave to come and pick up the kids, Claire said "I'm not going." "You have to go!" I said. "No, I'm not, I'm staying home with you," she insisted. I didn't know what to do. I could be in contempt of court if I refuse to give Dave the kids.

When Dave arrived, Claire told him she would meet him in the car, she had a bit more homework to finish. Dave, Grant and Hayley sat in the car waiting for Claire. Finally, Claire bravely ran out on the porch. "Daddy, I'm not going with you tonight!" she called out. "Have a good time." She waved and ran back in the house. Boy, she has guts. Interestingly enough, Claire's migraines went away after Dave moved out.

I am still teaching the doll classes at home. I can't get a real job because I can't leave the kids alone. Especially Grant, who started a fire out in the backyard the other day.

I still love sculpting my dolls, but I'm not making enough money to survive. I joined a divorce recovery group, even though I'm not legally divorced. I met the neatest woman, Shelley; and we've become friends. And she listens patiently as I prattle on about kids and divorce.

Leslie, my attorney, is GREAT! She's a good old southern girl and very smart. During the separation trial when Dave was on the stand, talking about how he takes care of the kids and buys their food and clothes, Leslie said, "Can you tell me what size shirt Hayley wears?" Dave couldn't because he has never bought their clothes. Poor guy--- he turned red with embarrassment.

Still, this is just such a sad time. I never thought about or wanted to get divorced. I remember sitting in the marriage counselor's office last March when Dave said he hated being married to me and couldn't imagine having to live with me for fifty more years. God, that hurt.

Oh well, at least I have my children. They are the light of my life. And my friends and dolls are helpful too. All things considered, I guess I am pretty lucky.

April 10, 1997 - Claire

Today Katie is sleeping over. She brought over "Honey I Blew up the Kids" and "Harriet the Spy". I am so mad at Hayley. Katie and I play with our Barbie's and they were at a cocktail party. I will write more tomorrow. Goodnight!

April 11, 1997 - Claire

Today, "Sabrina the Teenage Witch" is on TV and we have pizza, my favorite stuff to do. It has started to rain. I'm glad that I'm in bed and not outside. Uh- oh, it's raining, coming harder. Today I got hit in the nose with a tennis ball. We pulled weeds from the garden. My parents are going to divorce. I'm trying to be happy, but it is hard to be that way.

April 22, 1997 - Claire

Today was picture day at school... I wore a pink dress that was pants, but it looked like a dress. Jennifer was getting on my nerves. Jennifer is my new friend. Good night.

April 28, 1997 - Claire

Today I'm glad that I'm out of school. I just hate the song "Say You'll Be There" by the Spice Girls. Hayley keeps playing it over and over and over. I am so tired of it. Goodnight.

May 3, 1997 - Claire

Today I went to Six Flags for my birthday gift. We rode the Scream. It's a roller coaster. You go up a high hill as big as a dinosaur and straight down a hill, it is so scary. Bye-bye for now.

May 5, 1997 - Claire

I got poison ivy on me. I'm staying home because of it. I like to hug my bear, Claire. Well, that is all I have to say. Bye-bye. I hate that song that Hayley keeps playing.

July 7, 1997 - Claire

Today was the first day of camp. Mommy and Linda were my leaders. We made name tags that were made up camp names. My name is Blondie. Bye-bye.

July 9, 1997-Margy

Oh my God! We have Girl Scout camp all this week. I think I am dead. We have to be up at the crack of dawn (7:00), be outside in this incredible heat (99 degrees with 100% humidity) and work with kids all day. Why did I ever do this? The only good thing is that Linda and I are Claire's counselors for the second grade group. The girls are so cute to see and work with. But dear God, I don't know if I can live through two more days.

Claire is so cute, she believes in fairies so much. She and her friend Kathleen, have been making fairy houses and looking in the yard for fairies. Claire has talked Kathleen into trying out for swim team next spring. Kathleen seems excited about it

I'm still battling back and forth with Dave about the divorce, still in limbo. Will it ever end?

October 7, 1997 - Claire

Today I had to rewrite a story because Mrs. Voss made me. Mrs. Voss is my teacher in third grade. She is very nice. I had gymnastics today. I thought I had a tennis match. I'm glad I don't have one.

January 20, 1998 - Claire

Today was just a plain normal day. In the evening we let our dogs out, Annie and Five. I brought Five inside. Then Hayley and I went to go look for Annie. My mom went to pick up my brother at Boy Scouts and found Annie dead on the street. Annie was hit by a car. My mom told us when she got home. My heart broke in two. I knew that something had happened. I was so sad. I broke into tears. Everyone loved Annie. No strangers in her life.

January 20, 1998 - Margy

My beloved Annie Rose was killed tonight by a car. I still can't believe it. As I drove to pick up Grant at Boy Scouts, I saw her laying in the road. I got a towel from my neighbors, Sandy and Tony, and put her in their garage until I brought Grant home. I told Grant on the way home, and he became hysterical and screamed so loudly in the car, that I couldn't focus on driving. I had to scream for him to get control of himself. When we got home, I told the girls and we just cried and cried. My heart is breaking for all of us.

January 21, 1998 - Claire

Today was Annie's funeral. My friends, Amanda and Kristen came to her funeral. Everyone cried except Kristen's little brother. Grant was crying. I was hugging Mommy.

February 19, 1998 - Claire

Today we are going on a trip to Chattanooga, Tennessee. This is our first trip in one year. Grant is being a real nerd. Other than that, I am happy. Here we go!

February 27, 1998 - Claire

We got a new puppy. I can't believe it. Her name is Tinkerbell. She has a black mask around her eyes. She has three spots on her back.

February 28, 1998 - Margy

Yesterday I brought home our new puppy, who we named Tinkerbell. I love having a puppy in the house. They are so full of life.

I went to the Toy Fair in NYC last week and bombed. This, plus getting my hours cut at Craftworx (the ceramics place that isn't doing very well) and losing Annie has made for a tough couple of months. The divorce is still pending. But Leslie (my lawyer) is hopeful that it will be done soon. I hope she's right.

Claire is going to need braces next year because she has a crossbite. And the left side of her face hasn't grown. The orthodontist said this was pretty common in kids. It's so odd. Grant has horrible things wrong with him, but Claire gets these weird things (like when she was three years old and had to have surgery for a wandering eye, or when she had high blood pressure when she was five years old.)

May 22, 1998 - Claire

Today I woke up and saw my gerbil Chipper, was not moving. He sleeps in my room. I ran to my mom's room. I said, "Chipper's dead." She woke up immediately and said, "Is he?" I told her I thought so. She said; "He died in peace." We had a funeral. Max, Ray, Mason, John, Jake were there. We said "Rest in Peace" and buried him next to Annie. I am so sad about his loss. He was my first pet.

June 28, 1998 - Claire

We got a new gerbil. His name is Rasco, after Rasco in the "Rats of NIMH." He looks like Chipper. He's so cute. I love him. He sleeps in my room. He fell asleep on me. He is funny and only a baby. Uncle Chuck is visiting and leaving tomorrow. I don't want him to leave. I am just about to cry as I am writing this in my room. Night-night diary.

July 5, 1998 - Margy

The divorce was finally final in June. I can't believe it. We had to go through mediation. I'm tons in debt; and don't kow if I can afford to keep the house, but I am FREE! And I have full custody of the kids. They see Dave every other weekend and Wednesday night, from 5:30 until 8:00 each week. I'm thinking about substitute teaching at the school this fall. Shelley keeps encouraging me to go back to nursing, but I don't want to leave the children that much. And to be honest, I still have hopes that I can make it in the doll world, even after bombing at Toy Fair in February. It was only the first time I bombed; I did so well in previous years. I think it was because I went to bigger dolls, instead of staying with the miniatures ones. I guess my future is in "little" not "big."

I think it will be fun subbing and the pay is good, plus I'll be with the kids, on their schedule.

Yesterday was July 4th. It is the best holiday for the kids. Claire and Hayley dressed up Five (the dog) in an American Girl cheerleader costume. She won Best Pet at the parade. Five just sat there in her red, white and blue and looked precious.

After the parade, we went to the pool, where the kids swam all day, came home and had a big cookout at our house. Then, our neighbors the Lytles, spent about $1000 on fireworks and shot them off in our cul-de-sac. It was so exciting to see the fireworks close up and my children loved it.

I am teaching the American Girl Camps this summer at my house. I have ten kids in the morning and ten in the afternoon. They have so much fun making crafts, dolls, going on walks, learning about American history. I wish I could do this all year round, but the market is only during the summer.

I joined a singles group at church, and there is this one guy I kind of like. His name is Jeff, and I think he likes me, too, but he also likes another woman, Susan. Well, why shouldn't he? There are about twenty women to one man in the group. Still, it's comforting to be with other single parents. I've talked to Jeff several times on the phone. It's so weird to be sort of in the dating game again, after being married for fifteen years.

October 11, 1998 - Claire

Tonight I'm listening to the Weekly Top Forty. I just finished a game of manacala against myself. I was watching "Lost in Space." I'm like so bored. Claire Nelson

November 18, 1998 - Claire

Guess what? Today during our read-in, Matthew smiled at me. Love struck, Claire Nelson

January 13, 1999 - Claire

Today Dad was so sneaky; he took us to his counselor. WHEN HE WASN'T SUPPOSED TO!!!

February 22, 1999--Claire
Two days until my birthday. I am sick. I hope I can go to school tomorrow.

February 25, 1999 - Claire
Right now I'm at Dad's. The time is 10:40. At last it's 11:40. I'm scared. This place creeps me out. It's small and I hate it. I want to go home. I miss Mom and Tink. They said it was quiet there. Oh well.

March 12, 1999 - Margy
It's been a busy year. I still teach my adult doll classes on Tuesday night, work at the middle school clinic two days a week, and the rest of the week I substitute teach. Still, with all this work, I'm still in debt. Even though Dave pays alimony and child support, it doesn't come close to covering all the bills. It's looking more and more like I may have to go to back to nursing. UCK! Pray for a miracle!

I really shouldn't be so negative about nursing. I loved ER nursing for the first ten years. Then I just got so sick of all the politics in the hospital, the patients that weren't really sick, the homeless, the winos, the drug addicts. I was burned out and became cynical. I never want to be that way again. After I was married, I loved working at the clinic in Alpena as a school and clinic nurse, but those jobs are so hard to find, and don't pay well. Still, if I ever have to go to back to nursing, I'll go back to ER. I find it the most exciting form of nursing, you're challenged and you have to think on your feet all the time.

I love working at the middle school clinic, and substitute teaching. There is so much energy, positiveness, and helping of the kids. I work with this great lady, named Bonnie, who I really like, and she has been so kind to me. When I first came to the school, I was so beaten down after the divorce, but, Bonnie helped me get my confidence back.

Grant is doing okay. He's in eighth grade. It's been kind of hard to see him with his peers. I give all these ADHD kids their medications every day. And they are all friendly, talkative (obviously!) fun to be around. Then Grant comes in. He won't talk, kids tease him, and he ignores them and always looks mad. It's not just because I am in clinic either, he is always like that.

One day it hit me like a ton of bricks. Of all the learning disabled kids in the eighth grade, he is *the worst one*. He has no social skills at all. It's as if he is so far behind, he doesn't even get that he doesn't get it.

After all the socialization classes, counseling, etc, nothing has helped. So, I started reading the books at school and learned that besides his speech problem (dyslexia) his ADHD, his asthma, he is also mildly autistic. This is why he's so socially backward, and doesn't like to be touched. I asked his special education teacher, Mrs. Jones, about the autism, and she said, "Oh, yes, I thought you knew that." No, I didn't and it would have been nice if someone had told me. She went on to say "In fact, if he had been born twenty years before he was, he would have been institutionalized." I stared at her in horror. She said, "Well, think about it, he had his own language (his dyspraxia that we had him treated for when he was three years old) he is dyslexic, has ADHD and has no social skills. They would have classified him as retarded." How sad. To have put that wonderful, creative mind behind bars!

I talked to Grant's counselor, Dr. James about what Mrs. Jones told me and he agreed. But he said, "Grant is not retarded, he is learning disabled. He will do okay in life. He will never have a lot of friends, but he will have some. And he will have a job. Don't give up on him. He has great potential, but we won't know what that is until he's about twenty four years old. It takes these kids that long to grow up."

So, then I felt a little better, I guess.

Hayley is in sixth grade and doing great. She has friends and loves school. She and Claire love clothes and love to go to Old Navy to buy them (it's such a treat because they are better quality than Wal-Mart). She is still in Tag Classes. Go figure, one kid in sped, one in tag. At least I use all the accommodations the county offers.

It's kind of funny. Claire can't wait to get to middle school in two years, so I'll be there. Hayley is embarrassed that I'm there. But that's natural for her age. I love that I can be in the same school that Hayley and Grant are.

Claire is doing great in fourth grade. LOVES school, her friends, brownies. Everyday is such an adventure to her.

Money continues to be a big problem, especially now that they are in school activities, which costs money. I'm looking into getting a job at Home Depot for the summer, or somewhere where I can get health benefits, because my cobra insurance runs out soon.

May 17, 1999 -Claire

Mom says we can hardly afford this house. I hope we don't have to move. That would be so sad. I bet people's parents that aren't divorced are loaded with money. I'm scared. What if we move? What about Amanda, Katie, and all my friends? I wish I could help. Please don't let us leave. Save me!!!

May 29, 1999 - Claire

I will forever treasure this money. My grandpa gave it to me. He is very nice.

June 28, 1999 - Margy

Well, it's a gift from God. I've been working part-time in the paint department at Home Depot. It was kind of fun to mix paint, advise people what colors to use with what (me, the person who has to consult the color wheel to know this.) So, week two on the floor, I am lifting up one of those big five gallon paint cans, and pull a muscle in my neck. Besides having severe neck pain, something just clicks in my head: this job isn't going to work out. They want me to work hours when the kids are home, the pay isn't that great, and now I've injured my neck.

I was so depressed on the way home. Then, the principal from Taylor Rd Middle School called. They have an opening for a full-time learning disabled teacher's assistant this coming fall, and they want me! I'm so excited. We can get through this summer with the camps and all, and then in the fall I can take this job! Hooray!

Oh, another Grant story. When will they end? This spring, he got it into his head that he wanted to build a damn over the creek that the kids cross to walk to school. Grant built such an incredible damn, that the water stopped flowing through it. I kept telling him that this wasn't a good idea, but would he listen? NO!

So, finally they're having "Green Day" at school, where they clean up the environment, and their project is the creek. Grant drags me there, at 8:00 on Saturday morning and there is the principal and assistant principal talking about what a travesty has been done to the creek. How whoever built this damn has **changed the flow of nature.** Their goal for this earth day is to tear the damn down. I am embarrassed beyond words and if looks could kill, Grant would be 6 feet under right now. Finally, he goes to the assistant principal and admits to her that he was the villain that changed the flow of nature. She was a lot kinder than I would have been.

June 31, 1999 - Claire

You do not believe how bored I am. I'm a little bit tired. I have a swim meet tomorreow (I think I spelled that wrong) Furby is talking (yes, I have Furby). My Tamagotchi is asleep. Sometimes I wish I could go back in time and see everything.

Time Travel

What a plain and beautiful, not sunny day. It was raining. How boring. My mom was out. My brother was on a date and my sister was at a sleepover. So, I went into my room. I noticed it was different. I did not have a lava lamp or for that matter, a mirror, telephone, fan, bookcase. Instead, I had a war dronca, small plain lamp with ballerinas on it and a tiny mirror. I was so hot.

THE END

July 2, 1999 - Claire

12:10 I'm so nervous about the July 4th parade tomorrow. I dressed my dog Five up as Martha Washington. I hope she wins. Too tired to write.

July 4, 1999 - Claire

Five won the 4th of July Parade!! She looked so cool as Martha Washington, she even let us put glasses on her. She was coolest dog there

September 9, 1999 - Claire

I am sleeping over at Juliana's house

October 9, 1999 - Claire

Today Rasco got out in the laundry room and then when I got home from school, I went in and saw that he was dead. The most horrific sight. I screamed (while Mom was dealing with a roach) and fell into the post sobbing and kept sobbing until Mom took me out and we had to throw Rasco away. Tonight I couldn't clean out his cage. I was so used to seeing him moving, but there was nothing

October 1999 - Claire

Today we went to Disneyworld and MGM in Florida. I rode the Tower of Terror. I was so terrified I only screamed once and it was a small scream. Wow, I was scared today. We went to Magic Kingdom. I got to go in Mickey Mouse's House and rode "It's a Small World." Bye-bye DisneyWorld. Wah Wah Wah Darn!!!

October 30, 1999 - Margy

Today would have been my seventeen year anniversary, if I was still married. This year as a "unanniversary present" I had my ears pierced for the third time. Last year, on my first "unanniversary" I had my second piercing. I guess if I keep this up, I may run out of ears.

Things are going pretty well. I LOVE my job at Taylor Rd Middle School. I enjoy the people I work with and the kids. Everything but the money, it still isn't enough to pay the bills. Dave's alimony payment has gone down (since we have been divorced two years), and with growing children, and them getting involved in debate, cheerleading, football, etc, expenses just keep going up. But, God provided me with this job, so I trust that something will work out.

Grant is in high school, and that's not going too well. He just doesn't get it, even though he is in team-taught classes. He trys SO hard. He WANTS to make it more than any kid I have ever seen. Working with all these LD kids has helped me be a better mother to him, I understand him better, but it still can't make him do well in school.

He actually has two friends. The first one, Merrill, has an odd history. He's one of three boys and their parents committed suicide in front of the boys. Then this couple of professional clowns adopted the three boys. (I couldn't make this up!).

Saba is Grant's other friend. His mother is supposedly a nurse, but she's never home, so he's always on his own. I have a funny feeling about these kids, like maybe they could be or are already hoodlums. But I try not to judge them. However, I hide my purse when they're over.

This is the first time Grant has ever had friends. I'm glad now that he hasn't had any before this. With the LD crowd, the more LD, the more they tend to be wild and misbehave. And since Grant is at the bottom of the pile, he hasn't got the greatest group to choose from. Still, it is strange to see him with friends. Every once in a while, I'll pick up the phone to make a call, and Grant and Saba will be on it. Their conversations are hilarious. Neither one can understand the other, because they don't speak clearly and they talk way too fast. Grant will say "Do you wanna do somethin' tomorrow?" Saba "What?" Grant "DO YOU WANNA DO SOMETHING TOMORROW?" Saba "Whadiyousay?" Grant "What?" This goes on and on and on.

Hayley is good, she loves seventh grade, TAG. She's growing up to be such a beautiful young woman. And she's happy. She reminds me of the way she was before the divorce. It was like she had it all, and knew what to do with it.

Claire is a bundle of energy and life. Always on the go. She wears even me out. She is doing all year swimming, cheerleading classes (so she can try out in the spring) acolytes with Hayley at church, girl scouts, ballet, tap and contortionist classes. She's just fun to be around.

Claire in her contortionist class

September 25, 1999 - Claire

Why me? I had a sleepover at Amanda's and mouthed off to my mom! Now I'm in my room because she sent me here. Imagine a mad, serious face and that's how I feel. Mom: "I don't think that's cool. I go to long lengths to be a good mother. I did not bug you at all last night and I didn't do anything, just simply asked you if you wanted French toast!" (We were SUPPOSED to have cinnamon rolls, which I love) then Mom finished with "All I wanted to do was to make a nice breakfast!" Save Me!

October 1, 1999 - Claire

I wish Juliana liked me as much as she likes Allison. Sarah likes me. Now Sarah hates me. She used me to get Juliana back. Great trick

Title: American Girls

My American Girl dolls come to life. We visit "I Dream of Jeannie" in her bottle. Her bottle has pink and purple beads all over, and a pink sofa that goes around the bottle. We all talked and spent the night. The next day we went to Candy land—it snowed! We played on all of the candy things—it was awesome. Then we spent the night at Jeanne's again.

October 20, 1999 - Claire

Today we got a new gerbil, Rocker, after the Braves player, John Rocker. He is grey and sweet. I love him; he's the best in the world.

January 26, 2000 - Claire

I want these new pajamas from the (Limited) and guess what? Today Mom said she was going to get me pajamas from Target but I said, "Limited." She said I couldn't have them because they are too expensive. She said if I got them at Target, I could pick them out myself. Abuse?

February 8, 2000 - Claire

Whatever! Today I flunked a science test. Tonight Grant called me "dumb." I started to cuss and yell. I hate him. He is so dumb; he skipped Homeroom and is grounded.

March 10, 2000 - Claire

It's me diary. I miss Dad. I wish I saw him more. His house gives me a sense of old-fashionedness and comfort, which feels good. Dad is a nice guy and I miss him.

March 24, 2000 - Claire

I got to take the Tag Test. My dream.

April 30, 2000 - Claire

I was giving Mom a permission slip for something and she goes, "You're spoiling this TV show for me. Now go to bed. I will do it in the morning." I'm mad. I don't get to spend a lot of time with her. I made it into TAG!

September 2, 2000 - Claire

Dad moved to Washington, D.C. You know, I thought his family was over his work, but I guess not.

September 9. 2000 - Claire

I have a very secret notebook that has mean things about Hayley in it and she read it. Also, I read Hayley's dairy, and in it, she absolutely hates me!!! She isn't talking to me either.

September 11, 2000 - Claire

I tried apologizing to Hayley, no good. She is mad about it. I could write anything I want, she said, but she would put a good face on it for Mom. But, will she ever forgive me? Why must I have a mean older sister? I wish I lived in Sam's house (my best friend) and then Hayley would not be my sister. I would never have to live through this, but why must I? I wish she would just forgive me. Why doesn't she? Oh well, I will know never to write a notebook again.

September 11, 2000 - Margy

Claire was writing in her diary when I tucked her in tonight, and it reminded me that I haven't written in mine for a long time.

Where to start? I am back in nursing, working at Piedmont Hospital ER and North Fulton Hospital ER. It was so traumatic to get back to nursing. I had to take a refresher course last year, December; two weeks of classes and scheduled a hundred twenty hours on the floor at Piedmont. Horrible to try to get down there (30 minute at least commute) and arrange my hours around the kids.

But it's over and I'm actually glad to be back in nursing. After all the fears, could I remember the medications? Take care of acutely ill people? Could I think in a professional setting when I've spent the last fifteen years with children and no job? It feels good to be back. My ability to multitask is still there, as is my ability to help people and make them feel better. The pay is also enough to make the house payments and, hopefully, get me out of debt.

My first day back in nursing after 15 years was just what you'd expect. I walk in to work with Barb, my preceptor, and we are working from 11:00am to 11:00pm. Our first patient is a man who had been off cocaine for 7 years, but this morning took an overdose because he was upset about the death of a friend. He is unconscious, low blood pressure, not breathing. Within in ten minutes, we have intubated him, two IV's, foley and stabilized him. I kept hearing this little voice saying "Welcome back! It's like you never left."

Piedmont started me out at minimum wage for RN's, because I had been out of nursing for so long, but at my three month evaluation, Merry (my boss) said I had done so well that she gave me a great raise and put me where I would have been had I been in nursing all those years. Now, they are training me for relief coordinator-they think I have leadership potential. ME!

I'm divorced and at peace, finally. No one to hate me, ignore me, criticize me. I miss being married but enjoy having my soul back. I still worry too much and get scared about things, but when that old panic starts to set in, I stop. I weigh through my options and try those instead of feeling sorry for myself. I lived through a painful divorce, I can get through almost anything, I think.

My children, continue to be the joy of my life! I'm so grateful that God gave me these three people. I look at them and remember them as babies and toddlers, and then little children. I love them with my soul. I am so blessed.

September 19, 2000 - Claire

I wish I were smarter. I have to drop out of Tag Math because of my low grades. I hope I do better in regular Math. Meanwhile, on the Hayley front, she is still mad at me. Grant and Hayley were talking about how Brittany Spears is a slut. That is the last thing I would ever think about her. I wish I was an only child, and then I would not be bullied by them. I shall never have a notebook.

November 24, 2000 - Margy

Today I showed the girls pictures of me growing up. It was wonderful to share with them. And to me, looking at myself as a young girl—I was pretty. I never knew that.

I've changed my name to Margy. We have to put our names in the computer, and they only have room for 5 letters. So, I am sick of "Marg" and I wanted to do "Margie" but that was six letters. So, I was trying to think of what to do when it hit me. Take my name "Margery" and take out the ER (duh, I'm in ER) and leave the rest and I get a five letter word that is "Margy" for the computer. I like this name. It's kind of a combination of Margie (when I was little) and Marg (the adult and married person), and Margy, the new person. It just feels right.

November 26, 2000 - Claire

Wow! I have not written in a long time! For Halloween, Sam, my best friend, and I were twins. Sometimes she gets really annoying but she can be really sweet. I had turkey day on Wednesday, with the Graces, because Mom was working on Thanksgiving. Thursday we went to the O'Malley's. I spent the night with Erin. Horrible. I called Mom. I left Erin's house in the middle of the night. Erin was really tired, so I looked at her junk after she fell asleep. I wanted to read her diary but could not find any. No flashlight. YUK!

My teachers are: 1st period, Homeroom: McKinney. 2nd: Science: Durocher 3rd: Vogus, it used to be Mrs. Casey, but she's an assistant. 4th: Goldberg, super nice 5th: Lunch. 6th: Math, Snapweed. 7th: I have had Mrs. Smith-Hullman, who was Ms. Gay. And Coach Meehan for PE. Mom's birthday is in less than six days. Whew! That felt good getting it off my chest, which is very large, nuh uh! I have been noticed by boys, asked out and I said, "No" like Brittany Spears, I have been used by friends. History repeats itself. First Sarah, now Kimmy. "You're friends with Sarah, but you're unpopular. She wants me back because I'm popular." I think Kimmy is pompous. I have five gifts ready. Three for Mom, one for her birthday, stuff for Christmas, two for Hayley, one for Dad. None for Grant. I'm tired, that was a lot of info.

November 27, 2000 - Claire

I don't know what to write. I am now reading the book "Roll of Thunder, Hear my Cry". I feel like drawing.

Lying Smile
"Sure Mom, I would love to do the dishes"

"I hate you"

Defeat
"I would love to clean my room."

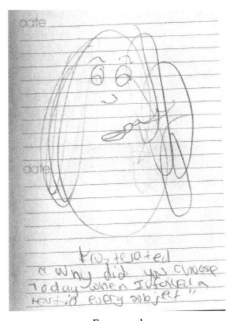

Frustrated
"Why did you choose today when I flunked a test in every subject."

Surprise
"What? Dad, you're moving to Washington?"

November 28, 2000 - Claire
Adventures of Shower Girl
The homework project adventures take over.
She was trapped in inescapable walls. Still wet from her shower in the cold rain. Giving her only a bed and skinny blanket.

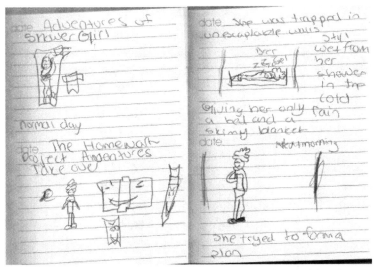

She tried to form a plan. Forming a plan... She did her homework and......she went home to her warm cozy bed.

December 7, 2000 - Claire

I just remembered what a suck-up Victoria Monroe was with Mrs. Puffy. She even wrote a story about Mrs. P's phone number. .Tomorrow I am going to the festival of the trees with the Girl Scout Troup. Am trying to be more popular.

"Susan's Story" by Victoria Monroe

"I went into the old house with my friend, Polly. We opened the door and a nice lady named Mrs. Puffy, with her beautiful brown hair, let me and Polly in for tea. She is my new best friend." Uck!

December 27, 2000 - Margy

Another Christmas. This holiday is hard when you're divorced. Of course, it wasn't a real picnic when I was married, either. Maybe Christmas is just hard, like all the counselors say.

The kids were with Dave until Christmas night. I missed them so much. Our first Christmas apart. Sometimes I feel that life has been unfair to me. To have gotten married when I was over thirty years old, then have a husband who was depressed and a son with all these continuing problems. Oh well, enough self pity, when I have so much to be grateful for.

My children are growing up healthy and whole. I hope. We discuss issues, we are open, honest. Grant has settled down; he's becoming more perceptive of social issues. With God's help, and a lot of letter writing on my part, Dave has become convinced that Grant needs a special school, too.

Can't remember if I wrote this, but Dave moved to Washington, DC in September. Still with the CDC, (Centers for Disease Control) just a different job.

Anyway, what convinced Dave that Grant needed a special school was when I wrote to him about Grant's friends at Chattahoochee High School, who are in special education with him. The first one, Merrill saw Dave's $700 bike in Dave's apartment and told him he tuned up bikes. Dave, thinking he could get a deal, (and also wanting to help the kid) asked Merrill to fix his bike and he would pay him. Well, Merrill stole the bike and lied and said it was stolen from him. Right! Also, Merrill's older brother is in jail for drug dealing.

Saba, Grant's second friend, has had to leave the state because he stole a car and it was grand theft auto. If he returns before he is eighteen, he'll be arrested. Then there is little Tim, who is so sweet, and not smart, has failed ninth grade twice, and will drop out when he is sixteen.

Anyway, we are using Grant's college fund to pay for him to go to a private school for learning disabled children next year. Dave is flying in so the three of us can look at these schools in March. I know that this is the right thing to do. I know that Grant won't graduate from high school, otherwise.

Grant is such a good boy and he's so bright. This summer, we switched his meds and he went on Zoloft. He told me that for the first time in his life, he could feel "happy." He never knew what "happy" meant before. How sad!

Hayley, my Hayley. She is such a mix of Dave and me. She has her Dad's intelligence, his calmness, his logic, his fear of social situations, his cynicism. She has my optimism, my sweetness, my helpfulness, my hardworkingness, my thoughtfulness and my desire to please. It is an interesting combination, but it should serve her well in her life.

Right now, she's so pretty and shy. I worry about her because she's so alone, yet I know she will be okay. Hayley has an inner strength, an ability to adapt that she doesn't even know she has. I got her in as a football trainer last year, and she has done well, although the first year was difficult because the other girls didn't like her. Finally, this fall, I had to be cruel and tell her that her shyness made her look like she was ignoring everyone, that it made her look like a snob. Hayley heard what I had to say, and changed, and became more open and friendly and now gets along with the other girls and the football players. This coming summer, she's excited about lifeguarding. She is such a wonderful daughter, and person. I hope her life is good.

And Claire—Claire is Claire. She is the child most like me. She has my unbridled enthusiasm, eternal optimism, my passion, my love of life. She has always just loved me. When she was little, she would crawl out of her crib to sleep with me. Grant used to call it "Daddy's side of the bed, and Claire's side of the bed."

The only sad part is to think that this must end someday. My children will be grown and gone. That will be hard. I'll be alone again. Pity party time.

January 18, 2001 - Claire

Mom is always tired and cranky, like tonight. I was just taking my usual long shower, when she goes, "Claire, get out of the shower." I had not even washed the conditioner out of my hair! "I want some hot water," she said. Then I was like, "If you want to take a shower, the water is not very warm." Her: "Well, I wanted some hot water; all I want is to just sit down during Smallville and not take a shower in the middle of it." Me: "Sorry, you should have just told me." Her: "Well, you know I take showers in the evening when I work!" Then I left. Now she is going to call her friends and tell them the story, saying I am selfish little brat! I hate it when she does that. The B*t*H

February 23, 2001 - Margy

Exciting news for me, I've been telling Hayley for about a month that she would make a great doctor. She's so smart, logical, and empathetic. What a wonderful combination! Anyway, she told me that last week, this boy at school was saying that he wanted to be a doctor, and she thought to herself, "Well, I could be a doctor, too." I said, "Don't you remember me telling you a few weeks ago that you could be a doctor?" and Hayley said "Oh, Mom, I wasn't listening to you!"

But it is so neat on so many levels. #1. Hayley has a plan, a goal, so even if socially things aren't good, she has a greater good she is working toward. #2. She has picked a career both her father and I would be proud of. I always wanted to be a doctor, and Dave is a doctor. I'm so excited that my daughter is going into medicine.Something that has been such a major part of my life, and my daughter might one day share! I'm ecstatic!

February 24, 2001 - Margy

Claire's twelfth birthday! I still remember her birth (c section) and how she started crying before the doctor had even gotten her out of my stomach. And how they immediately handed her to Dave and she stopped wailing. I always remember Dave saying that that was the first and only time she ever stopped crying when he held her (probably true)

Who would have thought that twelve years later, she would be such a wonderful gift! I so enjoy her. God has been good to me.

I still have some regrets about my divorce. I feel that Wayne (our marriage counselor) didn't really help us very much. I regret that the children had to go through the pain of divorce. Maybe there was something else that I could have done to keep my family together, but I know that my kids are better off now.

But I did love Dave and I wanted us to stay together. When we were first married, I loved being with him, I thought he was the most incredible person. I can still see our first house in Alpena, Michigan, with the wood paneling, the dated 70's colors, and the view of the lake from the windows. At night, I used to lie next to Dave and put my hand on his leg, as though in doing that, I could always keep him next to me.

March 13, 2001 - Margy

Crazy week! Sunday I worked in the ER from 11:00pm until 7:00am to help pay for Hayley and Claire's extra expenses, cheerleading, etc. Claire called, she couldn't sleep, she had a cold. (Mommy guilt). The next morning, Claire is too sick to go to school, but I send Grant and Hayley. I finally go to bed at 9:15am but the phone rings several times. It's Grant, he has forgotten his paper and I need to drop it off at school. I wake up at noon, Claire is still coughing. Time to go see Dr. Springer. On three hours of sleep, I drive she and I to Lawrenceville

(26 miles), and see Dr. Springer. We rush home and I drop off Grant's paper at school, then put Claire to bed.

I take Five the dog (who is having difficulty walking) to the vets. Drop off Claire's prescription at Eckerd's. Go back to the vet, who says Five has arthritis and gives me some meds for it. Get home at 5:15pm, and make dinner. Then, Claire and I go out to deliver Girl Scout cookies. When it's time to head off to work the next morning, the car won't start, the battery is dead! Have to call Tony, my neighbor to give me a jump. Finally, the car is charged and off to work I go in, exhausted.

April 28, 2001 - Margy

I feel like I have reconnected with Claire. During the last several months, I've pushed her to be with her friends, mainly since she is the only one with friends. And yet, I miss her when she is gone.

She wanted to skip school and spend a Friday with me, so, I took the day off. We had lunch at Cheeburger Cheeburger (she chose) and she got a manicure and pedicure and then we went home and played dolls.

Both us got lost in the fantasy when we were playing. This evening, Claire told me it was the best day she'd ever had.

Today, she and I went to her swim meet. Every event she swam, she would come up and hug me afterward.

Claire is such a delightful child. So spontaneous, such determination, a survivor. When she didn't get on the cheerleading squad last week, she bounced right back. Today, after the swim meet, we played dolls again. I know she is almost too old (twelve) for this, but still it's fun while it lasts.

September 11, 2001 - Claire

The Day when Fear was the only thought throughout America. Today will be written in history as the day NO ONE will ever forget. Today 2 Jets from American Airlines struck the World Trade Center and the Pentagon in Washington, DC. I know in many years I will be reading this to my children, but I will never think what I have thought today. I keep imagining so many people dying and our family locked in our basement. I wonder if today is the last day I will be living a normal life? Will we be not allowed to evacuate our own homes?

Will this affect America's economy? Hayley said she saw (on TV) other countries cheering and celebrating. Is this the end of life as we know it? I know I have a Social Studies project to work on; but I can't concentrate. Airports are closed for the first time in history. The president is who knows where? He wants war. I just want to know who would have so much hatred and psychiatric problems to do that to the U.S.A.? I feel so awful about the two people who called their families on the cell phones to tell them about the hijackers on the plane. All we can do is pray and hope God answers our prayers.

October 10, 2001 - Margy

Life is crazy. Grant is at Cottage School and in the eleventh grade. I have to drive him and three other boys once or twice a week (in other words, every day I have off). Hayley's in ninth grade and in debate and loving it. She has practice almost every day after school and tournaments on the weekends. (lots of driving for me as well). And Claire is in seventh grade and doing year round swimming, girl scouts etc. Plus, I work three to five days a week, depending on our financial need and my schedule. Still, with all this craziness, I think my life is very full and a lot of fun.

November, 2001, New Diary - Claire

Pets: Tinkerbell (dog) Lilly (bunny), Patches (bunny) Sequoia (bird) Parsons (bird) Scarlett, Tara, Ashley (birds).

November 4, 2001 - Claire

Dear Diary, I guess I will write in you every day. Get this, for Thanksgiving, Dad is taking us to Panama City. I miss Erika, my cousin. Guess what we did this summer? Travel to the NORTHEAST! My cousin, Erika, and I were having our periods, but it was awesome. At Dad's apartment, we chased Brett and some other guys. It was awesome. I used to like Tommy Martin, but he's gay, annoying and knows that I like him. On Friday, Donald Singer was really sweet; he made fun of me because I spelled "Kenya" wrong. He sat in front of me. Then, as we exited the door, I pushed and shoved him. I was like, "I'm sorry, Donald." He says, "You, I can forgive." Perfect English, huh? If he were to ask me out, I would say yes, because I am not Lisa. Everyone knows she likes Donald except Donald.

Did I tell you that in French I got moved to the back? Corey and I talk the whole time. He's really funny, but gay. Abby says twenty of her friends have crushes on him. What odd friends, I think. Donald kind of likes me. I want to say, wait two years from now, I will have beautiful teeth (when I get my braces off). I am glad Donald likes me.

November 5, 2001 - Claire

Dear diary, you missed it in Social Studies. Mrs. TJ was handing out brads, and I was getting the last brad. She asked me to get the other package off her desk. So, as I went up, I flipped my hair and smiled at Donald the whole time. My hair was flipped perfectly! Almost like a model! Then, I brought the box to her and FLIPPED MY HAIR again! And smiled. Here is my list to PROVE Donald likes me:

**he teases me and I tease him
**we compare grades and compete
**Friday, he moved and sat near me and talked to me!
**kind of cute

Okay, I like him already. We are friends. I guess I wish we were more. I see him at lunch. Once, he asked me if Jim and Mike were gay. I was like "Jim and Mike are not." Donald is in a reading group and has to sit with those losers in Reading. He calls himself smart. His name means "World Ruler". He is so much taller than me, if we got married, our wedding picture would be so cute. GOSH!! He is so hot!!

Maybe tomorrow he will like me with my hair down. It would be fun to kiss him. It would be fun because he is hot, tall, sweet, kind, and sexy and makes me happy. I can imagine it!!

I LOVE DONALD SINGER! He is just SO HOT I hope he asks me to the dance.

November 6, 2001-Claire

Oh my gosh, today was a milestone! Sam, (my best friend) and I had our first fight!! She was talking about how Egbert told some people she liked him. I could be sympathetic if I wanted too, but I have heard about Egbert for the last 9 weeks!!! So, I was trying to tell her my story about Corey, but she tuned me out!! I was furious so I started a lecture. I asked Sam how many of the guys she liked had ever asked her out. THEN, Kristen goes on about how Nick asked me out and Sam starts listening to her. So, I go "Kristen, shut up." Then I went on about how I hate Sam talking about Egbert. Then, Sam just walked around by herself. Oh, poor Sam. Then she called me and said she would not talk about Egbert anymore. I was thinking the damage had been done. Gosh! And I go "Ok." And she was like "Are you tired?" I was like "Yeah." Not. I am mad. Why Claire? Because I was telling you a story and you totally turned it into one about Egbert. All you care about is Egbert. Forget me. I wish I had said that. I said "Do you know how it feels to be tuned out, it's like the person is not with you. Look, I'm sorry." (At that point, I gave Mom the signal to call me and said I had to get off the phone)

Second Milestone!! I held a guy's hand. Ok, Corey kept taking my pens so I would put my hand out saying, "Give it back" and he would put his finger there and I would grab it. Then he would grad my hand really hard and squeeze it (like in Haunted House). This would go on for a while, and then it hurt. And, finally, he gave the pen back to me. At the end of class, he took my pencil case. So I go out the door and run up to him and go "What's up, Corey?" And he hands me the pencil case.

Oh yeah, Mrs. Bowman switched our seats and he was like "You stole my seat." Me "Well, you stole mine, too." She knows we talk way too much. Then at lunch, I was telling Stephanie K how annoying he is and she says, ""He's flirting with you. He likes you!" I could scream. Corey likes me!! No way! She said he likes me! Why would she say that? Me? Then, I realize he does. We tease each other, write on each other. And I took his pencil, chewed on it and gave it back, he took my pen, chewed on it and gave it back and I chewed on it. I knew he had slobbered on it, but I did not care. Then, I ask him, "Did you chew this?" He goes "Yeah." I was like "Ehh!" And put the top on so I could chew it. He draws on his leg every day. Today he drew on his legs with my pens! I do not like him, but I do like him. If he were to ask me out, I would say yes, but I really do not think he likes me or does he? Too bad Julie missed my story! Hah! See ya tomorrow!

November 7, 2001 - Claire

I was mad at Stephanie K. We were passing notes and she was like "Corey likes you." I'm like "Why? Who cares?" Then, she is like "Either you ask him or I will." And she asked him and he was like "Hell, NO!" Thank you, God! She was like, "He is lying." She kept asking him and he goes "Freak off!" I was devastated! But afterwards, I realized that it did not matter. Corey is trustworthy. He did not tell anyone I liked Tommy. I hope he doesn't tell anyone this. Anyway, I did try my hardest to be nice and talk with Julie. I just cannot believe she tuned me out. It is either Egbert or me.

Now, back to me and Donald. Today, Mrs. TJ was saying how when a government is overthrown, it is named after the new leader. For example, she said if Donald was the new leader, he would call the country "Singer." I turned around and smiled. He smiled back. We always make eye contact and smile. We are friends.

November 8, 2001 - Claire

Dear Diary, Not much happened. I was moved in French. Corey and I sit across from each other. We watched the dumbest movie. The substitute teacher was a freak. Except Donald kept turning around with one eye to look at me. He kind of smiled. Either he thinks I like him, or he is slow. He does have a cute haircut. He gets annoyed when Kara puts her pen on his neck. Donald and I are so meant for each other. I am playing volleyball with Stephanie, Pilar, and Gabby. It will be fun, I guess! I have to swim 9 events next weekend. I am going to die! Tomorrow is fitness day. I will not be so good.

November 10, 2001 - Claire

Today, Mom and I went to the Atlanta History Museum. It was fun.

November 11, 2001 - Margy

Claire and I went to the Atlanta History Museum. It was so much fun. She is just the neatest kid. Actually, all of my children are pretty neat. Shelley and I talk about our children on the phone. Her son, Josh, is Claire's age, and Jake is four years younger. We have such a great time exchanging stories. I don't know what I would have done without her the last several years. She is the best friend anyone could have.

November 11, 2001 - Claire

Today we went to church. The appraiser came to the house, because Mom is getting it refinanced. My room looked beautiful.

March 11, 2002 - Margy

You know, all of my life, I've tried to figure out what life was about---to understand myself and those around me. I felt like if I could figure out life, then maybe I could learn from my experiences and go forward and help others, or at least not make the same mistakes again.

But after all these years, I guess I have decided that life just happens. It doesn't mean anything special, you just do the best you can with it. I don't mean to sound cynical, it's just hard to believe that life has a special meaning. But now, I realize it's just luck and you can't do anything about it.

Hayley is in Debate! Of all things, her teacher asked her in September if she might be interested in Debate, because she had such an aptitude for it. And we talked about it and she joined it and has LOVED it. It has been the best thing for her. She was looking for something, and now she has found it!

My dad called today. He is really scared. Never thought I would hear that from him, he is always Mr. Macho. He thinks Mom has bone cancer. Such odd feelings, I have. So many years ago, I used to be so mad at her, and yet, the last few years, my parents and I have made peace. It's just scary to hear my Dad sound so old and scared.

May 22, 2002 - Claire

Field Day! Wednesday, today was so much fun! I played cooperative games, tug-of-war, hula hoop and water sports. Although my group got disqualified in water sports we played four square. After a while, I decided to be Todd's partner. I messed up the hit, we were out. Then it was time to walk over to the soccer field and Todd followed us and sat by us. We got popsicles and I dropped mine (accident) and he gave me his. EWW! So I bit off the end, and was like "Does anyone want this?" And then Kevin goes, "I bet Mitch or Corey does." I went "Oh my God, shut up!" Then Todd goes "I'll take it." I was like "Ok, whatever." And then I told Todd I was sorry about he and Michelle (breaking up) because I was. Then I saw Mrs. Pip talking to Mr. Thompson about me, I go "Oh shit" only Coach Morgan comes by at the exact same time and says, "What did you say?" "Shoot." Coach Morgan, "That's what I thought."

May 23, 2002 - Claire

Guess what? (in the bad way) Todd likes me!! Yeah, listen to the story---he called Pilar last night and said, "I like someone." Pilar: "Who?" Todd: "Do you want me to tell you now or later, because my Dad needs to use the phone." P: "Later." Then at school, Pilar asked, "Who is it?" T: "I don't want to tell you." P: "Please give me a hint?" T: "The first name ends with an 'E'. Last name ends with an 'N'." So, I thought me or Stephanie Gordon. So then he said "I think she knows". Pilar: "Why do you like her?" Todd: "She's nice and is the only girl I think won't reject me."

Stephanie K---turned him down in 6th grade

Pilar - turned him down in 6th grade

Kayle - turned him down in 6th grade.

Lauren - turned him down in 7th grade

Ali - of course she turned him down. She is way too popular.

Michelle - turned him down Wednesday.

Likes me - I......Oh well, see ya tomorrow and he is going to ask me out tomorrow.

I am going to reject him but listen to what I will say. "Todd, you're a really nice guy, but I am not allowed to go out with people. And I would rather be your friend instead of Girl Friend." Then I might give him a hug, maybe. Bryan was really annoying me in Language Arts (I came from Mrs. Boyles) and sat in Mrs. Shoemakes class. He would poke me, talk to me and draw on me. He wrote on my foot "I love Bryan," then in my yearbook wrote a sweet message.

May 26, 2002 - Claire

Here is what happened on Friday.....I went to school and had fun until 4th period when I, Pilar, Andy, Simon, Paul, Lisa, and Johanna decided to play Truth or Dare. Some secrets were put out. Then, in the hall as I was walking to 5th period, (I was near Pilar and Todd) Pilar goes "I dare you to hug Todd." So I did! I pushed through a whole crowd of people and go "Todd, I want a hug," and I grabbed is neck and put my head on his shoulders and he grabbed my lower waist and smelled my hair and then he let go, then I did.

Then, after our hug in Spanish class, Todd told Pilar thanks, thinking she put me up to it. He was so happy. I could not believe he hugged me back. He smiled the rest of the day. I could still not believe I hugged a guy who likes me. I am so nice!

After hugging Todd, I hugged Bryan. Then I played Truth or Dare in the French. It kind of turned into me, Bryan and Christina. Then in Social Studies, (after lunch) I played charades. Then in Math, I fell asleep watching the movie, "Stand and Deliver." It was boring and in the hall, at the end of the day, I walked up to Todd and hugged him again with my eyes closed. He, of course, hugged me back.

June 1, 2002 - Claire

Hey! Today we went shopping for a book to read while being on vacation with Dad. We went to Chapter 11. Mom had to preview the first book I picked out. It was about turning seventeen. She looked at the back and was like "This is a little old for you." This made me really embarrassed! So the next book I picked was "Girl Interrupted." She read it and said, "This is for older teens. Hayley, what do you think?" Hayley read some pages, and then she was like "It seems dumb." Then Mom goes "I don't know. I don't want you reading junk and growing up too fast." Then I was like "Mom, please can I just try it?" Gosh! I mean who cares what Hayley thinks? I was mad then. Mom: "Are we ok?" Me: "Yeah." Mom: "I just think, you know, you're mad at me." Me: "Nope."

June 9, 2002 - Claire

Church. So I am wearing my "KISS ME" shirt and orange skirt. Mom: "I don't like that on you." Me: "Why! I am only acolyting, I'll have the robe on, and no one will see it!"Mom: "It doesn't belong in church." Me: "No one will see." Mom: "Take it off!" F*ck you Mom!

July 6, 2002 - Margy

Time is much too quick for me. This summer has let me know that. My children are on their way to being grownups. I'm so proud of them and so sad to think that my life as a parent is almost over. This part of my life has truly been the most wonderful and rewarding.

Grant came home tonight after a week with his father. He never called once all week. I told him how sorry I was about the accident. He said, "What accident?" I said, "The one where you broke all your fingers." He said, "I didn't break my fingers." I said, "I thought you must have or I know you would have called me." He got it eventually, I think.

Between Grant's job at Pike's Nursery and Hayley's job as a lifeguard, I have not had all my kids together all summer. Hayley had a two week debate camp, Claire had Girl Scout camp and cheerleading camp and Grant was with his Dad.

Claire is going to be a basketball cheerleader in 8th grade. I am so excited for her. I hope she has a wonderful time. Grant and Hayley were NEVER into sports. This will be a new experience. I can't wait.

I don't know where time goes. Grant and Hayley are already leaving me, and soon Claire will, too.

Dave is moving back to Atlanta in August, and my Mom is sick (though it's not bone cancer, like we thought) and has had to get a pacemaker. I think that big changes are coming. I hope I can handle them.

Claire's 9th grade cheerleading picture

July 18, 2002 - Claire

Hi Journal, You are the only notebook I can count on. Since Hayley has been back from debate camp, she feels like she is better than me. Like, she told me not to pay so much attention to the dogs. I only do that because she always hogs them. And she's saying bad words.

I miss school. It is so cool knowing that I am going to school as a cheerleader. I got my swim team trophy. Hayley really thinks she's cool. And Mom is just, you know, ignoring my headaches, not letting me buy the clothes I want and books, anything I want. It is annoying.

August 24, 2002 - Claire

Okay, on Tuesday this week, Todd called and asked if I could go out with him. I said I couldn't because I'm not old enough! Oh my gosh! I totally lied, which I totally felt terrible and what if I go out with someone else? On Friday, it was terrible. I got my period on Thursday and on Friday, and I bled through my pants in 8th period.

I got moved next to Chad (Corey's best friend) and the shirt I had on says "KISS ME." So Harry and Corey were surrounding my desk and saying, "Your shirt is so demanding." As they were saying this, I realized I had bled through my pants, so I ran to the bathroom and got as much out as I could. And I told everyone it was chocolate. Corey and I talk across the room. Harry hugged me (I did not hug him back) I made this face and Corey laughed and I go "What are you laughing at?" Him: "At the way you're acting!" He smells so good too, but he flirts with Rachel Taylor. They would be an ugly couple. She is too punk rock for him.

Jennifer likes Corey. In class, Bob (her kind of gay friend) said he knows someone who likes Corey. Someone in the back of the class goes "I bet it's Jennifer," and Corey goes "I hate that girl." I felt bad for Jennifer; he does not like her at all. Jennifer said she thinks if you asked Corey if they were friends, he would say yes.

Maybe I like him, maybe I don't. I'm not sure. He has gotten a little weird. Although, he does kind of flirt with me.

Still, when I think of him and Rachel I think 'disaster'.

He was crowding me at my desk. Wanted to do what my shirt said. What will happen? I don't know; ask in a couple of days.

September 11, 2002 - Claire

Joined and dropped out of play "Oliver." Found out about NYC fame modeling tryouts. I didn't make it. I am still doing all year swimming.

September 17, 2002 - Claire

Here we go again with Todd. OMG! Oh My God]. Today in PE I was playing four square. Well, there were only four people left so he and his friends decided to play. I kept getting him out and then, he would, like give me his square. He still Freaking Likes Me! Wow!!!

We might get a new puppy. A girl for our dog, Carter. Mom wants to mate them. So exciting! My period is close. Well, sort of. It has been a long week. Tomorrow, cheerleading practice with Britney and Chelsea. Eww!! Oh well. CYA whenever. I'm really tired.

September 30, 2002 - Margy

Grant got his driver's license the first time! He got a 95% on the test! Of course, it was our usual drama to get there. We went to the DMV and stood in line for about three hours, and decided to try earlier the next day. So, we start camping out at 8:00. At 11:00, we have actually reached a human cop and he goes through Grant's papers and says Grant didn't get the right attendance paper from school. I am near tears. I have to work tomorrow and can't come back. And if Grant can't get his license, he can't drive to school. For some reason, the guy took pity on us, and said if we could get the paper, we could come back to the head of the line. So, Grant and I head off to Cottage School (fifty minute trip, one way) and get back to the license bureau about 2:00. The cop waves us through, but then Grant has to wait in line to take the driving part. But, he passed! Now, if only he doesn't get in any accidents.

So my six weeks of working nights so he could learn to drive to school (without carpooling), the $700 dollars I paid for driving lessons, and the used car I bought because he couldn't drive a stick shift - have all paid off!!!

Claire has to get braces again. Her teeth are going back to where they were. She was pretty upset, but it's only for a year.

I am in LOVE ~ I was in Petland and saw the cutest Papillion I have ever seen, and I knew that I had to have her. She just looked in my eyes, like she could see my soul. And though I have always sworn I would NEVER EVER buy a dog from a pet store, I bought her on the spot. We named her Ginger Bridget. And we all love her to death.

October 3, 2002 - Claire

Today was okay. Stephanie K and Pilar called. That sounds like something I would have said last year. It was great to talk to them. I had not heard from them all summer. They said they looked totally different. Stephanie has brown hair, Pilar has long hair. I haven't changed at all. I am more cheerleaderish, but not full blown. I haven't changed my sense of style because I didn't grow. It was weird to them what was going on because it was like they knew who I was talking about and actually cared. I've never had anyone care that much.

October 13, 2002 - Claire

Hey babe, Today, Grant and I are switching rooms. Mom found Grant's collection of porn and was furious.

I do not like Corey. I am sick of being absent from school and wished somebody liked me. But they don't and I need money, for shirts, shoes, jeans. I look like an orphan. I just ended my period. Well, almost. I'm kind of bored. Grant has made my room smelly and gross. I am still trying to get the smell out of his room. I'm gaining weight, but I'll lose it. I'll have a lot of work at school. I cannot wait for the games to begin for cheerleading.

October 17, 2002 - Claire

Hey Hon, on Tuesday, Jennifer came up to me and was like - "Corey likes you." I was like "No. He doesn't. He's going out with Jessie (I don't know her last name, but she has the large birthmark) so he can't like me." Jennifer: "Oh, I didn't know that."

(Less than 5 minutes later) Jennifer started talking to Corey and then I heard a little of their conversation. Corey:" She said what?" Jennifer; "That you were going out with Jessie." Corey: "Why is she going around telling people that?" (Then I got involved) Corey: "Claire?" Me: "What?" Corey: "Why are you telling people I'm going out with Jessie?" (I have to say I acted out the next part really well. Me :"(shoulder shrug): " I'm not, Why would I?" Corey "Oh, yeah" Then class began.

He might as well go out with her, they do everything together, and I mean everything. Their lockers are next to each other. So they walk to class together, they eat lunch, they buy lunch together, are constantly talking, probably call each other, and act like they are connected at the arm. SO WHY AREN'T THEY GOING OUT! BEATS ME!

Jennifer said she's going to Ben's party and they're going to play spin the bottle. Corey is going to be there. Oh Well!

And Jennifer said she that at Ben's party, the new kid, named Tim, will be there.In the beginning, I thought he was nice, then I was nice to him, but now he is just acting like a jerk, poking my stomach, kicking my butt, saying hi to me constantly. Oh yeah, and Z is always poking me in the stomach, too.... I am just getting so...I HATE THEM. THEY ARE MEAN, UGLY, COMPUTER GEEKS. BIG LOSERS. And so, I had a little outrage there, but I am good. I just really, really DON'T LIKE THEM!Another little space there, but I am good. I am babysitting on Saturday. And I babysat last night. Unfortunately, I forgot I was babysitting so I had to get dressed in under 30 seconds.

I think Johnny Donovan (the kid I baby sat for last night) is gay. My reasons:
** Not many 6th grade boys like to dress up for Halloween two years in a row as a girl,
** Not many 6th grade boys let their sisters do makeovers on them
** He likes speedos
**He shows no interest in girls
**He cares about how much he weighs.

Allen Lane is really nice. We're not enemies, but you know we have history. Well, more like he asked me out both years and many times. And I said no MANY times.

Back to school.....I have not found my social group yet, unfortunately. I still have problems making friends with boys. I probably have this problem because in my mind (or used to be) girls and boys only went out and were not friends. It's really weird. I know guys that flirt with me and I think??? You know I'm not extremely ugly or fat; I just need friends in my social class groups. So, I said a prayer to God. I go through this every year, and find my friends by Christmas. Like last year. I don't like even years in school, odd years are the best.

<u>Groups</u>
Smart kids (not high enough IQ)
Popular (never get there)

Weird (kids who don't bathe)
Sluts (no, no thanks)
Goths (black is not my color)
Girls & boyfriends (I'm working on it)
Girls only (kind of weird)
Geeks (I will not buy a $300 calculator)
S.P.E.D [Special Education] (I don't strive for it)
Cheerleaders (I will never get there)

I just need to find a group and I have a few friends now. Oh, Hey, I'm tired and I will see you later, my play went well, too.

I have been working hard to exercise and eat less. I've been so good. I hate those kids who eat 3 pizzas, 2 milks, 3 fries, and ice cream and gain one ounce. It's not fair. Mom just walked in. She has a problem with our dog, Carter. Sorry, now I'm under the covers, she made me go to bed.

<u>Reasons I don't like Ginger, the dog:</u>
*Yeah, she is beautiful, but that's it
*Mom treats her like royalty
*She's like a princess who is spoiled and gets all the attention in the world and is beautiful
*Everything she does, Carter gets blamed for it, and Mom really hates him.
*Mom compares Ginger to Carter, there is no way that is a fair comparison; it is cruel and stupid
*Mom even wants to sell Carter. He is like the "Beast" in "Beauty and the Beast". At least I love him.
*Ginger is a spoiled brat waiting for attention, wanting it all the time and never leaves you alone.

Sorry, but it is the truth. I needed to write a lot of things and get it off my chest. And also, today in Language Arts, I was reading the part of a boy and I said, "Yes, I am your step-father." And the whole class started laughing and saying things like, "Do you have something you aren't telling us?" It really got old fast. Whew! I really am going to be tired tomorrow, but, oh well, see ya later. Love ya, Claire

October 20, 2002 - Claire

I wrote a lot the other day. Well, yesterday we got our cheerleading uniforms. Mine looks good and makes me look thin. But today, OMG!

Mom makes us do chores every weekend, and so I chose vacuuming. So I just finished vacuuming and now she is re-vacuuming what I just vacuumed. And she's like "I don't like this attitude of yours, one bit, girlfriend." Two things wrong in that phrase. I'm not her girl friend, and I am really tired, plus my back hurts. So it's her problem, not mine. She so totally uses me to do stuff for her, it makes me really mad. Until later. Claire

The day turned out better than I thought. Mom and I went to the gym and then Mom, Hayley, Grant and I saw "Tuck Everlasting." It was so sad, because he asked Winnie to drink from the spring and meet him in 100 years and she didn't. She lived her life. He came back and saw her grave. It said "Dear Mother, Dear Wife." It was 100 years old. It was so sad. I cried constantly. Although, it was very good. Then we went to Rio Bravo. Until later, Claire

October 22, 2002 - Claire

I learned important news today. One minute......Sorry, Mom was coming in to tuck me in. Anyways, the Corey, Jesse situation (the hardcore facts)

* Corey liked Jesse and Jesse liked Corey

* Corey at the beginning of the year sat with Nicole, Jesse and Danielle

* After a while, they stopped sitting together

*I found out Nicole likes Corey, Nicole knows Jesse likes Corey and Corey likes Jesse, so she stopped being friends with her, for that reason.

*So, this week Jesse began to sit with Corey

*Corey kept asking her out, knowing she would turn him down, but with the signals she was giving him it was obvious she liked him, too

*So finally, she said yes, and I found out today they are going out

*So to conclude the story, Corey and Jess are an extremely ugly couple, Nicole likes Corey and Jennifer is very disappointed.

The End (touching, sweet?) Yeah, right!This isn't a fairy tale

Today in Social Studies, after Corey was talking to Jess, he came in and still poked me in the stomach and semi flirts with me (SEMI) Also I was like talking to Chad, and Corey counted how many times I said "like" in a sentence. So that really annoyed me, so tomorrow, I will not say "like" at all. I hope I can do it. Until further notice CYA Claire Nelson

THE END (please!)
This story is just beginning. More hard core facts about Corey and Jess
*Today I found out Corey secretly has a crush on Molly Rhines
*So now, Corey is going with Jess, but he has his eye on Molly, because he talked to her online, flirts with her in science (Kelsey Report)
*I don't know if he thinks she's pretty or likes her personality. Not too sure, maybe he doesn't even like her.
*Since I don't see Corey and Jesse having a future, like Nikki and Morgan, I think this relationship is meant to fail. So I think if Corey and Jesse break up, Corey will have Molly sit with him, than go out. Now I can see them having a kissing relationship.
*I do not see anything between me and Corey, ever, although I'm not that depressed. I see a thread of hope. But hey, a thread is what makes a sweater, right! I'm not kidding, but at least I tell myself the thought: One thread, one thread.
*Every girl likes Corey
-Jesse (Duh! She's going out with him)
-Nicole (very, very secretly)
-Molly (even though she's going out with Ryan)
The smallest thread of my whole body
See ya later. Claire (I may add on to the list)

November 7, 2002 - Claire

I know I have not written in a while, so let me clue you in on what's going on.
Things important that have occurred since the Last Entry
- My first basketball game. I got my hair done and I did my back handspring during the game and half-time. At the end, my hair totally fell out.
- Bryan and I have become better friends and we have everyday hugs!
- I like absolutely no one.
- I get my debate partners tomorrow
- I am anxiously awaiting my period (.) because the only other time I had it at school, it went through my pants.
CYA   Claire

November 11, 2002 - Claire

I'm in a happier mood, although I am waiting stuff. Like for instance, my period {.} Anybody reading this diary should note, I talk about my period A LOT.

We saw the movie "The Ring" yesterday, Mom and I. It was scary, but gory.

My period won't come. I am sick of waiting. I want it here. This weekend, I have 3 games, 1 Saturday because they are at the same time and 2 on Sunday. If I have my period on both days, it won't be fun. Oh well, my pen is running out. CYA

Claire

November 18, 2002 - Claire

So I'm having my {.} period and it is day 4, this weekend we had a game on day 2, and it was horrible. Every 5 minutes I would check to see if any blood had gotten through. I had millions of layers on, underwear, shorts, bloomers and skirt. After that, Mom and I got pedicures.

Today in French, I was talking to David, first name basis; he decided to sit in front of me. I was like ok. He passed me a note which we passed all period. In the note, we talk, when I asked how many hours he spent on the phone, he said 9, and then asked me if I wanted to be added to the "board" because I was jealous. I wasn't jealous, I was just wondering. So, then he was like, if you want to be added to the board, you can. I then said, "If you want to." So I gave him my phone number and he gave me his. We both put it in each other's hands. He called me at 5:30 and like we talked for an hour. Then, I got bored, so I said I had to go. Then I ended up calling him back at 7:00, so you know, I like him as a friend. We talked for 2 hours tonight. That is unbelievable; it has set a new record, at least for me. He asked me to go to the movies, but I don't know, I would only go if Jennifer would because I would not want to be alone. I will think about it. Till Later CYA, Claire Nelson

November 19, 2002 - Claire

Well, it's later, so I rode with Kelsey to school. And I saw Jennifer, so I talked to her and told her about everything. So, in 2nd period, David started passing notes with me and I really didn't want to. So in the note, this is the interesting part, he said "How long is cheerleading practice? Will you go out with me?" And I was like OMG! How could you ask someone that after only talking to them on the phone, but then I go to evidence--- Evidence:

*2 - hour conversation—when I want to be friends with a guy, they think I like them

*Talking about others

*I called him back

*I am just too nice

It hurts, what do I do? How am I supposed to stop people from doing this? I mean, yeah, he has the right to ask me out, but seriously, did he think I'd want to go with him? Did I show any idea of caring? You know this happened before and it will happen again. So I returned with (I was good) "Practice is 2 hours, no, I just want to be friends, why?" I know I have 3 million commas, but I was so smart. And I wish he wouldn't sit in front of me, so I couldn't have the chance to talk to, or pass notes with him. He returned with "Just wanted to see your reaction." I don't know the rest or care, but I wish he would back off. I THANK GOD so many times for not letting us have lunch together. Well, you know how he wanted to go out with me and wanted to see my reaction. Well, this is my reaction

Needless to say, the day did not get any better. So, I got home and I couldn't get myself together. I had so much extra steam to burn-off. I had to exercise, so I ran around Lynbrook Lane. Needless to say, the day did not get any better. So I got home twice to the song, "I've been

crawling in the dark, looking for the answer." My teacher told me to run when I have too much energy. I was definitely tired.

Want to know the lowdown on Candy? Okay, so Friday, Candy and Zach were in the electrical room for a soda, then he asked her out. They have technically been going out, but this is actually going out. So they started, you know, to get it on in the electrical room, so "Sparks were flying in the electrical room." I think that is funney. I can't spell. I swear my life could be either a show (soap opera, drama, or just a sitcom) or a book (a series that never ends). I know it would be famous around the world. I'm so glad I have a diary. Without it, I would be either stressed out or really weird. Oh, wait, I already am.

David invited me to the movies, but I never answered. I'm so glad I have cheerleading and should go to bed and stop thinking. Although I have cooled down since earlier in 7th period. I walked down the hall and freaked out. I felt like I was going to faint.

The 411 on Corey and Jesse I'm not sure but I don't really care. I don't think they are together and yet I don't care. I am surprising myself. I really better go. CYA Later, Claire Nelson

November 20, 2002 - Claire

Hi! I had a great day. David didn't sit in front of me. He thankfully got the point that I don't want to be friends with him. THANK YOU GOD! He and I pretended we did not exist. Jennifer said to him yesterday, "So I heard you asked Claire out?" He looked sad and was like "It was just a joke." I guess, so why ask me out? He was trying to cover his embarrassment. So, Jennifer and I were walking home. (Wait a minute, need to tell you something. Today at the end of French, we must have been late. So Bryan came in and was like "Hey Claire!" Yeah, I'm still in his class. And he came up to me, behind a desk, and gave me a hug. And Jennifer just stood there smiling. I said "bye" and left) Okay, so we're walking home and Jennifer's like, "I need to talk to you." And I'm thinking: Please, let it be good. Jennifer goes "Do you like Bryan? I mean because you guys like give each other hugs and stuff? You definitely seem like there is chemistry." (me thinking: well, sort of?) Jennifer: "I don't mind if you like him, just tell me the truth." So I'm like thinking, Oh dear God, how could she think I'm lying? Who lies to their best friend? How do I answer this? So I go (I answered this shaky but sure.) "Jennifer, I don't like him. Well, I don't really know. I don't think so. Otherwise, I would get all nervous and red in the face and shaky. You've seen me, right. I don't like him." She goes "How can you not know if you like him or not? You are so nice to him. I get nervous around him, and obviously, you don't. I still don't know or not. I mean, you two hug a lot." Me: "I'm not lying. (God, please get it through to her) I wouldn't lie to you." And I dropped it. I know for a fact I don't like him. You know, we're both on the basketball cheerleading squad and I'm sick of her.

Jennifer: "Well the coach is going to teach us how to tumble when we find a safe facility."

** She has a really bad round-off and I know for a fact that she will take forever to learn her back handspring.

Jennifer: "We can't afford Cotillion."

** Like my Mom can? My Mom just knows it's important to me. But Jennifer can afford to go shopping every weekend. And buy new clothes.

Jennifer: "We go to the gym so much and eat so healthy."

** If you go to the gym so much, why do your thighs look like they are going to explode with fat? Why do you eat so much if you are trying to lose weight? Do toning exercises.

Jennifer: "Ben, my friend, is so funny."

** Ben is so gay it is not even funny. He does everything so girly and feminine. He just needs to learn that Guys should not be that close to girls in the 8th grade.

Okay, so I have the right of opinion, don't I? That was really mean, but I needed to get it out. Wait, that's why you are called a diary, I love you! I know you are an inanimate object. That's okay. CYA LEIDA

I got my arguments for debate ready today.

A Day in the life of Claire Nelson

1. Walk to school—usually quite boring and tiring because I have to make conversation with Julie.

2. Arrive/Homeroom—Usually more entertaining than the walk and I see Adian and Morgan.

3. French—the usual, not that bad, I am very smart so it is semi-fun.

4. After French—Brian walks in, I give him a hug, make chit-chat as Jennifer and I leave.

5. Science---3ᵈ period—I have Chelsea S in my class, that should explain something. Ana is my friend in that class.

6. Health-- not too bad. Get to see old friends from 6th grade, material in class is boring.

7. Chorus--either OK or just plain long. Dr. Sibbley usually goes on and on and on about the play or something else.

8. Mr. M's Math--not only does Mr. M. put me to sleep, but he just cannot teach very well. I miss my old seat.

9. After Math--Brian usually walks in, give him a hug and make chit-chat, usually longer hug than first one.

10. Mrs. McC's -Language Arts Mrs. McC gets moods swings that just annoy me. I am doing well in her class and Morgan's in there.

11. Mrs. Jolly, Social Studies-- Debate, debate, and yes, debate. This woman lives for debate. She always has a debate story to share. Most of us don't care anyway, but we have to listen to take notes. I guess she's a good teacher.

12. Extended Learning Time-- Not Fun you say. ONLY 3 girls in that class aren't cheerleaders. Listen to these people: Shayna, Brittany, Liz, Lindsey, Michael A, Matt B, Stephen W. The list is horrible. I really don't like my class; it is really embarrassing when anything goes wrong with me.

13. Dismissal--FINALLY. I walk with Kathleen and see people I know. See Bryan and give him quick short and sweet hug. That's my day.

Today, I was talking to Bryan and Jennifer wanted me to tell him that she likes him. So I go. Me: "Bryan, I need to talk to you." (hand on his shoulder) Bryan: "Yeah, what?" (hiccups) Me: "Jennifer likes you." Bryan: "I know." Me: "Who told you?" Bryan- "I don't know, I don't know who I talked to." Me: "Oh, who then?" Bryan "I honestly don't know." So I gave him a pretty long hug and left. It was really Daniela (but she is obviously not very important to Bryan)—I am.

November 26 2002 - Claire

Last day of school for five days. I got tres' mad today. It was just gross. OK I should be happy for them, and I am but....

--she had her hand on his chair
--he had his hand on her thigh
--they are going to the dance TOGETHER

And oh—yes, they aren't even going out!! OMG!! I'm talking about Kelsey and Joe.

I don't really know what I was mad at, but I'm trying to figure it out.

Things I was mad about:

*Joe, Kelsey ---maybe, but why? They don't belong together. He doesn't like her, or does he?

*Maybe she can get a guy and I can't?

*She just liked him and he asked her to the dance, but she doesn't like him that much

*That was probably it. I don't feel good, more tired. I had a bad day.

November 31, 2002 - Claire

Last night of break! I was on line, and talking, you know! To Mary and she was saying how horrible her life is and I was trying to be cheery. But that didn't work. So she was telling me about her surgery. She has had so much surgery because she is fat. That is the only reason. And then she's like "Don't tell anyone, but I've been overdosing on Advil and Tylenol." and I was like "You?" She's like "Yes, don't tell anybody." So I was like "Got to go, bye!" (I was kind of freaked out about that). Guess I'll ask Mom what I should do Then, Kelsey came on and I was like on. she goes 'Who's this?' I go "Claire" so we were talking to each other and Michael came on. Kelsey left. Michael is like "Do you know Molly Rhaines?' I was like, 'Yeah, she is sweet, why?" He goes "No reason" I'm like "you like her.". He goes "No, what RU talking about?" Claire: "Admit it, you like her. You know it." Michael: "?????Who" Claire: "Liar, you know it." Michael: "Oh." Claire: "How long have you liked her? Michael: "Since last summer." Claire: "Are you ever going to ask her out?" Michael: "Will you?" Claire: "Heck, you're the one who likes her." M: "Don't know. Are you going to the dance?" C: Yeah, you?"M: "Yeah."C: "Are you going with anyone? (it took a while, so I thought he thought I was going to ask him to the dance. So to clarify. Claire: "I'm going to the dance with my friends." Michael: "Me too." Claire: "It's more fun." Michael: "Yeah." So we chit-chatted and it was funny, though in the beginning he didn't want to talk to me at all and in the end, he started the conversation. He He!I can so make anyone talk. I'm going to church with Kelsey tomorrow. I will be tired but, hey, it's worth it! I guess.

December 1, 2002 - Claire

Big week. Debate, French, DANCE-- speaking of, we went shopping for a dress and found one, bought it and I tried it on. Mom was like "Oh my goodness, sweetie, that dress is too tight, mature and....I don't want you wearing that." So I got the hint and she gave me a shawl. So I was getting in my pajamas and Mom was like "I want to talk to you about that dress. Either you wear something else or wear that shawl all night." "Fine, whatever." Mom: "Well, you can wear either." Me: "Fine, I won't wear it". Mom: "You can wear it, just with the shawl." Me: "Just return it and pick out something else."

December 2, 2002 - Claire

Debate tomorrow. I have a professional outfit, I straightened my hair (well, Hayley did) and I'm prepared. I know we'll do well. Today, I was talking about how we talked about gay guys in science and Bryan pinched my side and freaked me out. And then he grabbed me with both his legs, and wouldn't let me go. Finally, I was like "Please" and he goes "Okay." And gave me a very long hug. I let go before him. And that happened again this afternoon. But ok, whatever. I did not care. I'm nervous about debate, but I don't know if we are going to win. That was weird with Bryan. I'm not sure if he likes me or not, or likes hugging me, because of my boobs. Don't know.

December 6, 2002 the Dance! - Claire

I went to the dance with Cameron and Kelsey. It was semi-fun with Tiffany crying, and Stephanie G. trying to get guys to slow dance with her. I understand why they wouldn't want to. So she wanted Scott to slow dance with her but he said no, like a thousand times. So Stephanie G asked me to ask Scott to dance with her.

So I went up to Scott before the next slow song and said: "Stephanie really, really, really wants to dance with you on the next slow song." Scott: "Who?" Me: "Stephanie." (I'm guessing he didn't hear me and he said "You?" Me: "No, Steph." Scott: "I'll dance with you on the next slow song." Me "OK" (confused). He totally did not see the point in the conversation so the next slow song came on and in the beginning, he wasn't there, so I started looking for him. Now I played this smooth. I saw him walk around like he was looking for me and I pretended I didn't see him, just to see if he would come over to get to me. And he did. And we slow danced together. He was "I think Allen likes you," and I go "Please, don't say that, we have history. He has asked me out in 6th, 7th and please, hopefully not 8th." Scott: "Oh." Me: "Yeah." We danced with my arms around his neck. Me: "You agreed to dance with Stephanie." Scott: "Yeah." Me: "Why?" Scott: "I knew this would be the last slow song, so I technically can't dance with her." Me: "Smart!"

The slow dance was awesome. After it, Scott said, "See you on Monday!" And left. He is like 70,000 times taller than me.

All I know is I think Scott purposely didn't understand what I said. I may be wrong. Don't know. I'm glad. I know Scott just danced with me to be nice, which was really nice, but maybe he wanted to. He obviously didn't want to dance with Stephanie G. Hah! I got to dance and it was completely magical, and I slow danced with the first person out of the family. Claire. I am happy!

December 8, 2002 - Claire

I lost my voice on Saturday and Sunday (well, today). So all I could think about was slow dancing with Scott. Ahhhh... in a happy way. He is so sweet. To have danced with me was kind from the start. OK, he knew going into this that I must like him just a little.

Well now, I really like him. I have not seen him all weekend. Amazingly, it is the weekend. I just keep thinking about the one dance that was too short. I don't know why he decided to dance with me. I didn't even beg him. That was for Stephanie, but I got a dance out of it. I do like that he said, "See you on Monday!" at the end. And also, at the beginning, he was the one who found me when I really saw him first. Hah, I'm so smart. He He. I'm tired, I have to go to sleep and dream about Scott. He He!

December 12, 2002 - Claire

Almost a week since the dance. Since then, I got Scott's screen name from him, talked to him every day (I am good) and he so cannot stop looking at me! I talked to him on line and this is our conversation: Scott: "Who is this?" Claire "Who is this?"

Scott: "I asked first." Claire: "Claire."

Scott: "Nelson?"Claire: "Yeah. Who are you?" Scott: "Ben." Claire: At this point, I was like "Ben who?" Scott: "Baker." Claire: "There is no Ben Baker in 8th grade."Scott: "I live in Peachtree City."Claire: "How do you know me?" Scott: "Scott talks about you a lot, he really likes you.Claire: "Right, stop."Scott: "I am Ben." Claire: "SCOTT STOP!"Scott: "I am Scott." Claire: "Thank you. How did you get my screen name?"Scott: "I dunno." Claire: "What's up?" Scott: "RU okay?"Claire: "Yeah, why?" Scott: "You were sounding kind of crazy." Claire: "I have like 50 things to do. Scott: "Have you seen James Bond?" Claire: "No, but I want to. I was going to go this weekend, but we have a game." Scott: "For what?" Claire: "Basketball, we're cheerleading."Scott: "Oh. Cool." I had to go because I was actually talking to Morgan and he told me he likes me and I didn't want to tell him who I liked. Time to eat dinner, CYA tomorrow.

Okay, so today I wore Hayley's pink puffy sweater with puffy pink balls that hang down from the neck. I walked into Homeroom and people were laughing hysterically at me. It was like everything I had feared came true. And their like, you have fuzzy/hairy balls and they kept trying to get my attention. So they could make fun, but I didn't respond. I'm almost crying as I write this. So I switched shirts. I was walking down the hall when I saw Jennifer and she was, "What's wrong?" I told her the story. J: "I'm so sorry."Me: "I feel horrible." Jennifer: "I love your sweater. I almost bought it." Me: "People are going to make fun of me more if I wear it." Jennifer: "Don't feel bad, it's their fault."

So we came into French late and of course, I looked like I had been crying. I was crying on and off during the test. It hurt. Really, I hope that no one has to experience this. I saw Morgan later, after Homeroom; he was like, "That was so funny, we were laughing to death." This made me want to cry! I'm crying now as I write. That was so horrible and tomorrow I have to go to school and be nice to these idiots. That hurts all over and I'm really tired. CYA tomorrow.

Oh yeah, we had the Geography Bee and I had 3 questions left until I was out. I made it to the 7th round and it was me, Jessica, Greg and Will. Will, Greg and I got two rights. Then we had 3 more questions and Will and I got one right. Now, it's just us tomorrow. I had a question which was "What is the chain of mountains that is on the Pacific Coast? Ah! The Ring of Fire. The question I got right that got me my spot was

"What salty sea is located between the Red and Black Sea?" The Bead Sea, remember Social Studies last year! I had a question about the Silk Road. I don't care if I win or not. I'm glad I think either way I'm in. Don't know though. CYA. Maybe I'll be happier.

December 17, 2002 -Claire

OMG! I hate when Mom is like "Will you do my hair?" And I'm like well…and say no. And then she's like "You know that's too bad. I really wanted you to, and was counting on it." And she tries to make me feel bad. Then later, she's like "Look at my hair" and I'm like "It doesn't look that bad." She then says, "You know when you do things for others, it makes you feel better." And I'm like, "See, you're trying to make me feel bad." Mom: "Maybe I was." She told me not to worry so much about it.

I'm mad because Scott doesn't answer my IM's and like our umm… computer …it's screwed up. Yeah Right! I'm just so stressed about everything, it's all building up and I need to get it out.

December 18, 2002 - Claire

The Debate:
- My second constructive was amazing. I blew them away.
- My rebuttal was not so good, but Kathy's rebuttal was great. So we WON! Wow! I was so happy!!
- By the way, today, Bryan hugged me and was like "You smell good." Me: "Really?" Bryan: "Yeah, in the guy way." Me: "That's so nice." So again, I got complimented on my perfume. I don't know if Bryan likes me or not, so I am not sure. He definitely likes my scent, though. Night!

January 6, 2003 - Claire

Happy New Year! Ok, so here's what's up.

*Had period for December, not due for awhile.

*Dad moved back (eww! Sounds bad)

*Aunt Phyllis came. Went to St. Augustine to visit Aunt Shay and Uncle Peter.

*Lost my purse.

*Talked to Morgan and found out stuff. We are becoming, I guess, friends?

*I'm totally falling for Scott and I haven't even seen him in like 2 weeks.
*I'm having thoughts about Jennifer.
*Cotillion starts soon, see people I don't like.
* I don't know what to do with Dad

So now, you have gotten the 411. I'm totally confused. I mean not only do I have like 30 thousand things to do: school, cheerleading, cotillion, Dad, Scott, migraines, friends, tryouts....That is a lot! I like haven't been sleeping. And my migraines are really terrible. Dad, Hayley and I had to leave the theater 2 days ago because I had the worst headache and I was nauseous. It was awful. Not to mention, I have no idea what to do with Scott and how to handle it. I don't even know if he likes me or not. But I don't think so. I haven't built up the courage to ask him. Well, I haven't TALKED to him for 2 weeks, so I wouldn't know. And DAD, oh don't get me started. He comes back and expects us to be all loving and stuff. Well, he was the one that left us. And now, my schedule is getting pretty tight and he's like, "Do you want to get together on Wednesday?" I can't. You don't know how hard this it. It's like being pulled, which I don't mind, but it hasn't even started and I'm worried. January will be jumping.

January 6, 2003 - Margy

Another year! They seem to go so fast. Isn't that a sign of getting old? Oops! I don't want to get old. I want to stay right where I am.

Claire is a basketball cheerleader and doing so well. She is so limber and continually working to improve her performance. It's so much fun to sit in the stands and watch her. I have gotten to know Kelsey's mother Fran, better, too. (Kelsey plays on the girl's basketball team) So we sit together (with Mr. Tony, her husband) Mr. Tony teaches piano in the neighborhood, and Hayley used to take lessons from him. We watch Kelsey and the girls play basketball, then the boys play, and through it all, Claire and the cheerleaders cheer. Claire's getting ready to try out for football cheerleading at Chattahoochee next year. Hard to believe she'll be in high school in the ninth grade. Her migraine headaches have gotten worse lately, so I'll take her back to the doctor. She may have to go back on Imitrex. That's the thing that helped the last time this happened.

January 7, 2003 - Claire

I started out so excited, nothing could ruin my life. Scott totally highlighted his hair, it is like ¼ blonde and ¾ black. It could be worse. I totally want to go out with him and Kelsey is going to ask him who he likes. I will get really mad if he says "Umm...Claire, I think." And Mom just can't catch a hint. Well, I was like so mad because the Donovan kids were so annoying and bratty. So I was all bummed and she's like "Is your charm bracelet in here?" And I'm like "I don't know." Mom: "What is in here? Oh, who gave you this?" Claire: "Julie, Mom." Mom: "What are these hand stickers?" Me: "Stickers" (I sigh). Mom: "Don't get all snippy with me." Claire: "I'm not." Thank God she left. I love Scott!

January 12, 2003 - Claire

We had a game which was fine. But I had my shirt on, and Mom was like: "That shirt is too tight." Claire: Ok" Later…..Claire: "Mom, my shirt is not too tight." Mom: "Yes, it is." Claire: "How?" Mom: "It's too tight." What! My shirt is way not too tight. I hid it in my closet behind a dress so Mom won't donate it. Oh yeah, I don't like Scott anymore because I had Kelsey ask him who he liked. Kelsey: "Who do you like?" Scott: "Why?" Kelsey: "I want to know." Scott: "Stephanie Crook (I knew that) Who's asking? Claire or Stephanie?" Kelsey: (with a straight face) "No one."

Now that would have worked out if she didn't come and sit down next to me right after. Because Scott sat down like a table away and saw me. I think he changed his (IM) because he is never on. He's just really rude and thinks he's great. I'm sick of Erin at school, always trying to hang around Kelsey, trying so hard to exclude me. Kelsey is my best friend. It is unbelievable; Erin is never going to get rid of me. She is not using me to get to someone else. That is not going to happen again.

I still can't believe Mom thought my shirt was too tight. It didn't even stretch across my stomach. Oh well. That makes me want to wear it more, not around her, though. He He. I loved this journal. Yet, I need another one. Love ya, forever!Claire (end of purple journal)

January 16, 2003 - Claire

I know this notebook is really gay (Aunt Shay got it at the dollar store), but I had to write in something. Ok, so yesterday, I had Cotillion and like I knew Mike Parker would be there. He saw me and was like "How's it going?" I'm like "Fine." He totally did not remember me at all. I must look really different. So I got home from Cotillion and Mom was like "Unzip your jacket. I want to see your shirt." I know she's thinking that my shirt is too tight!! Luckily, the shirt was loose and passed. I was like "Why did you ask me that?"

In chorus today, Dr. Sibbley said someone was singing off key, and I guess I was. Dr. Sibbley: "Jennifer, which one is singing off key?" Jennifer: "I'm sorry Claire." Dr. S: "Okay, sing it one more time, Claire." I was bright red and embarrassed. You don't know until you are discovered to be the one wrong person in the soprano group. I was scared. Dr. S: "Look, she looks like she got her teeth whitened!" Because I was so red, and everyone was laughing. It was horrible. I was so red and my jacket was getting hot. So she had me sing alone. Now, I sang awful. Jennifer put her hands her over ears so not to hear me sing. It really hurt. As I walked out, I heard people talking, and that really hurt, too. I swear, though, that I will never sing louder in chorus, I will always sing at a whisper.

Also, Erin is starting to take over Kelsey. During Social Studies, they moved their desks closer to each other and exchanged notes. I almost wish Mrs. J would catch them doing it and move them. I feel so left out. And Erin thinks she is the greatest and is constantly combing her hair. She even asked me if I liked it. Dorkey! I'm so sick of her and she is in Cotillion. Claire!

January 30, 2003 - Claire

Hi Di! He He! Today I stayed home and slept in. Can you believe it on a Tuesday? I went to bed at 6:30. I had a headache and Mom gave me some migraine medicine. We also saw John Smoltz, the Braves pitcher, at Dos Copas. He He ! Guess what, well you can't, but here goes. Okay, so for class I'm supposed to be a freed African Slave for our firing line in Language Arts tomorrow, right? Okay, so I wasn't at school today. So I need some other info. The only person I could think to call was Chad, because I didn't want to call just anyone so I consulted with Kelsey and she said I should just call him and get it out of the way. So, here's our conversation.

Claire: "Hi, is Chad there?" Person: "Yeah." Claire: "Can I talk to him."Chad: "I am him." Claire: "Oh, okay. Hi, this is Claire." Chad: "Hi?" (in a worried voice, like I'm going to ask him out) If I was going to ask a guy out, it wouldn't be him. Claire: "I had a question about firing lane tomorrow." Chad: "Ok." Claire (I ask the question). Chad: "I haven't done any research." Claire: "Oh! really, but do you know about...." Chad tells me he hasn't even started our Language Arts project. Claire: "Oh, me either. Who are you doing?"

Chad: "The teacher in white mice." Claire: "Me, too! Ok, well, I have to go." (making sure to end and not get bored or run out of things to say.) "Alright, bye." Chad :"Bye."

So that didn't really help, but it's not over. During "Friends" (the TV show) he calls and here goes: Claire: "Hello (I knew who it was because Mom picked it up and was like "Who is Berry?" I mean, Perry?"(Chad's last name) OMG! And then she finally gave me the phone. Chad talks about how he found info and stuff, (I had said if he found any info to call me which wasn't an invitation to call me). So he had a reason. He gave me the info and I pretended I had to go. He has a really boring voice on the phone.

So, that is 3 guys who have called me this year. Fun stuff. I love ya' to Death .... Claire. I love Will. By the way, Will is mine ALL SUMMER!

February 17, 2003 - Claire

A month later! Let's get up to date. So last week I was sick with a cold for 3 days and had a ton of work.

Valentines Day came and I have a long Scott story. I forgot to get Julie a carnation and so I bought her a bouquet and I forgot to bring it to school. I felt so bad and I guess she thinks I don't like her or something, so I have a friendship to repair. That's just about it.*So, on Valentine's Day, I was just expecting flowers from all my friends. But low and behold....I got one from Scott!! Yes, Scott. It said: To Claire Nelson from Scott Mason. And I was like "Whoa!" I finally get over him, and he starts to like me.

Camryn said he does because hello! We slow danced together at the dance and we weren't even going out. She also said because he wrote his last name, it proved he wanted me to know he sent it. And also, to send someone a carnation, you had to find out their homeroom, and I did not even know he knew mine. I don't even remember him coming in and seeing him look in my homeroom. And he had to buy the carnation two weeks ago. But. silly old me (well, stupid old me) wrote "I heart Will K" on my hand. Big mistake. Scott seriously looked disappointed when he saw my hand. So, then I felt bad, but realized I had to get over Scott. It's not like he sent any other carnation to girls. And how should I know he would send me one? It's not like we're good buddies. I think I think too much. I'm just so confused. I don't know if I like either of them or not. Scott asked me what my screen name "Tnkdancer" meant and I told him and he printed it. I'm tired. Good Night! I am also confused with Scott, but I don't know.

January 29, 2003 - Margy

God spoke to me today. I don't know how else to describe it. Dave has moved back to Atlanta, and I've been so upset because he has bought a house within walking distance to the school! (in Shelley's neighborhood, of all things) He's already telling the kids that he wants them to come over after school. I feel such fear and loss. My children are all that I have and care about. Oops, the old abandonment issue. I have wrestled with this for several weeks. Then today, it was like a light went on. I knew I would be okay. That God would take care of me. That He is always with me. I realized that my children may never get another chance to live this close to their father. And they need to be free to make their own decisions, to see him, not because he guilt's them into it, or I guilt them out of it, but because they want to. It was all so clear and I knew that God is there with me and will look after me.

February 18, 2003 - Claire

So, I went to school and we had a fire drill and I was in short sleeves. So I looked around and only Scott had a jacket on. So I was like "Can I borrow your jacket" and he gave it to me! And I was warm! He just handed it over. It was down to my knees, so cool! Abby said she talked to him and she was like "You should go out with Claire." Scott "No, I like someone else." So you send me a carnation? I'm lost.

February 24, 2003 - Margy

Claire's 14th birthday. She and Dave went to Montreal for the weekend, and had a great time, but were supposed to be home yesterday. Because of the snow, they won't be home until tomorrow. I can't believe she isn't here. This is her first birthday without me. It made me so sad. Shelley said I shouldn't feel bad, it isn't a big deal, it's just a birthday. But it feels like so much more. For her to have her birthday and I'm not there, it isn't right.

February 25, 2003 (red hearts on white fur journal) - Claire

Starting a new journal is like staring a new chapter of my life. Yesterday was my birthday, probably the worst of all of mine. So here is how our weekend went.

Dad took me to Montreal for my birthday.

Friday: **We catch a plane. Dad was on high profile list (because he works for the Centers for Disease Control in Atlanta) and had to wait 30 minutes to get approved, make it there to find our hotel alright and go to bed.

Saturday: **Wake up at 6:00! Go skiing and stop around 3 because I got a headache. Go to hotel. Freshen up: and go to dinner at 9:00, five courses and finish at 10:30.
**Force Dad to go to Hard Rock Café and buy me a shirt for my birthday.
**Get lost on way home, fall asleep in car and finally get to hotel and fall asleep in 30 seconds.

Sunday: **Wake up at 9:00 and am very sore from skiing. Check out of hotel.
**Go downtown and visit Dad's friend Carmelle (she ended up breastfeeding at the table). She was very nice and pretty.
**Then go to cathedral, which was very beautiful and large and very Gothic (you know the time period)
**Get to airport in Montreal, try to get through because now both Dad and I are on the "High Profile List" and had to wait a long time. This is where we made a HUGE MISTAKE, and I mean HUGE. In Atlanta, you know how when they check the bags, there is this scale and you just leave your bags. Well, we just left our bags and went to Customs. Apparently, you're supposed to bring them through Customs. OOPS!

So, we got on the plane and just sit there. I, being smart, do my homework. There was TOO MUCH fuel, so they had to take some off and then the refueling tank broke, so they had to get another one out there. And, then, they finally got the weight out. So then they had to de-ice the plane. We started to go over to the gate, when the power went out. The left engine of the plane just broke. So then the plane had to be towed to the gate. And we did not have our baggage because they said it would be on the later flight so....
**We then went to Customs to have them find our baggage because neither flight had left and there was not any way our baggage had gone anywhere. We sat in Customs for like an hour and they told us to wait until tomorrow.

**So, we had to find a hotel for the night, yet we still hadn't eaten dinner, so went to the Game Plaza and got a room. Left my one carry-on baggage there and went to find a place open at midnight.

**We found a place and I had a cheeseburger and fries. There was like nothing open, so I was just happy to eat. I was hungry.

**We got back to the hotel and I took a short, quick shower. Then we went to bed. We had spent 7 hours at the airport.

<u>Monday</u>—my Birthday

**My birthday actually started at the burger place at midnight, but hey! That's okay.

**Woke up at the time science class started and ate breakfast at the hotel

**Took a cab to the airport, sat, waited, (our flight was delayed) and was really bored. Got on plane, read "Girl with the Pearl Earring" cried some and then we got to Atlanta.

**We went to baggage claim and we saw our luggage and we were so happy. Then we rode Marta which was when I realized that that was my worst birthday ever because it didn't even feel like my birthday. Then we drove from North Springs and that was my weekend.

<u>Today</u> -- Went to school, felt loved and I guess Jennifer is not mad. Not sure. I'm so confused about Scott. I walked in and he's like "That new girl is hot. She's got a nice butt." and I probably had this face on "Ewww" Then later, he says to me, "The whole school knows who I like." So, I got in the hall and I'm like "It's kind of funny that the whole school knows who you like and yet, she doesn't." And he's like "Really?" And I'm like "Yeah." (you loser, you sent me a carnation, not her!) I'm like so confused: does he like me or her or both? I don't know.

Doctor Sibbley said I didn't turn in my permission slip for festival and I don't know what to do. Should I run and turn it in tomorrow or the day of festival or just blow it off? What will she do? If I don't go, will she assign me an essay? An essay is not that bad! I think I'm just going to blow it off, but I don't know.

Mrs. Kran called for a babysitter and she was like "I can't remember which family it was, but there was this one time the babysitter said she could be out late but then she had to go home because her Mom wanted her home. And I was like "Oh yeah, that would be me, (Mom had said

I could be out late, but not until 2:00am. Who doesn't come home until 2:00am?) No doubt she probably didn't forget, just wanted to be nice.

February 2003 - Claire
Did Cotillion and swimming.Lily, my bunny died.

March 2003 - Claire
Was assigned my 30 page paper, more like 50. For one week I went to bed at 2am each night. People started to notice my obsession about Donald and made remarks. Unpleasant ones by the way.

March 12, 2003 - Claire
The Claire and Scott decision

Evidence: It is so obvious. He gave me a carnation on Valentine's Day! OMG. The kid will let me do anything. I borrowed his jacket, necklace for 2 days, he lets me do or take anything, he always looks at me in the hall! He is like so sweet! He always, you know, makes sure I know he's there (like I don't)

What he knows: Duh! It's obvious I like him. I mean ok, not only did I ask him to dance, but you can tell. And like last time when he knew I liked him, he was, you know, cocky about it. When Kelsey asked him who he likes, he answered but then was like "Who wants to know? Stephanie? Claire?" Of course, I was the one who wanted to know. Embarrassing, right? I invited him to my party. Not like the loser has answered, but, hey, that (um…..) Final decision:The Jury is still OUT

March 23, 2003
Life is so crazy, I don't know where to start. Grant is graduating in two months. I still can't believe I wrote that. He'll go to Gwinnett Tech in the fall for landscaping. He's still trying to find a job, since he got let go from the nursery. Hayley is busy with debate and doing outstanding. She keeps winning first speaker and all these three feet high trophies. Claire is doing cheerleading, and all her usual other activities. A few weeks ago, her best friend, Kelsey, and Kelsey's adult cousin, Courtney, took them to the High Museum of Art (as part of an eighth grade project). Claire had such a great time with them. She really likes Courtney, says Courtney is just like me. This weekend,

Claire wanted just she and I to go to the Coke Museum (still the same project). It was great fun. She's at such a great age to go places with. I hope we always stay close.

April 5, 2003 - Claire

A lot has happened since the last time I wrote. Okay, so I had my birthday party. Chad and Morgan came and we played "ManHunt." It was fun. Then we had the 8th grade field trip. I will explain about that. So, on Thursday morning, we all had to be at school by 6:00am. And that was early, so I woke up, got there, wanted to sleep on the bus, but Kassi was singing, so NO WAY! We went to a ton of places and that night we stayed at Best Western. Kelsey, Stephanie and I were up until 3:30 and then, well, Tiffany fell asleep at like 12:00, so then Kelsey gave me a back massage and took a picture of me. (I look stoned in the picture) and somehow Corey got hold of the picture. Stephanie, Kelsey and I all fell asleep in the same bed. The next day was busy, but fun on our way to the Okefenokee. I heard someone was going to ask me out. I didn't know who. I found out Chad really liked me and was thinking of asking me out on a roller coaster. And I kind of liked him and Scott at the same time. Cause at my party, Ali was all over

Chad and I kind of got jealous and he didn't care that Ali liked him. Also, I thought he liked me because he did come to my party. So, at the amusement park he was like "Come ride this roller coaster with me" and I was like "Oh, oh, ok." When I sat down he wanted to sit next to me, but the seat was broken so he couldn't. But through the whole thing, he was talking to me. And yelling to me. I didn't see him for the rest of the night, but at the end, I found him and he told me all the roller coasters he rode and how many times. I kind of got bored, yet acted interested. And then, later that night, when we had 2 rooms (one Kelsey and I were in and Steph and Tiffany were in the other). Tiffany calls and says that Chad called and she gave him the room number, and he was going to call.I talked to him for like 10 minutes and then talked to Corey and Scott for an hour. He has trouble making conversation with me because he likes me so much, I guess. So the next day we got back and I watched "Legally Blonde" on the bus, which was great. The night we got back I went to bed at 8:30. I was really tired. All this week I have totally wanted him to ask me out, but he doesn't know if he wants a girlfriend. So then, I wasn't sure if he liked me or not. I asked Corey and he said he does, but doesn't know if he wants a girlfriend. And every person I talk to about this says he is so nice and sweet. I just want him to ask me out!!

Right now, I'm at the beach on spring break in Panama City. Of course, like all Dad's vacations, he made us a home-cooked dinner. And of course, we all complained about it. Goodness, it is only our first night here and he has 3 more dinners. And he totally thinks I have an eating disorder. Well, I had a milkshake before dinner, which was really smart. And he's like a 50 year old pouting; real mature. Huh! And Mom got mad at me because I didn't do the laundry, but I had to teach the little kids tryouts all week and I was not here. But she's forcing me to get my hair done. And Dad is a baby. Hayley thinks she is biggest hooch ever. And she's on the Debate team! And Grant is just himself. Me, I'm just here, waiting to go home. Everyone is here from college and I'm really bored. There is no way I am going to hang out with Dad. Out of the question. So, this is my spring break? Fun? Want to join me? Love ya, and save me.

Claire

April 2003 - Claire

Grant was sent home on a bus due to being out until 3:00am. We didn't know where he was and he came home drunk. I met Logan, Stan and someone else. They fell for Hayley's breasts and then we took a walk on the beach and they hit me in the butt and really liked it. They started to like me, but getting rid of Dad was hard. I had my period then. I tried out for cheerleading and on the night when Mom picked me up, I said "I made cheerleading!" And I did. I am a football cheerleader!!!

April 28, 2003 - Margy

So much is going on! Grant graduates from high school in May. It's so exciting. We're going to have the biggest party ever! I never really believed this day would come.

So, story #1—I hadn't gotten Grant's senior pictures taken because he wouldn't get his hair cut, and he doesn't have a tuxedo. But I was getting nervous about it because Grant has a retainer with the false front tooth that he has had for years. I have been afraid something would happen to that tooth before we got the pictures. I have visions of my southern boy without a front tooth.

Grant finally agreed to have his hair cut and I made the appointment for him.

Kathy, at work, loaned me her son's tuxedo jacket. Wednesday night (four days before pictures) I get home from work with the suit and Grant is standing there, looking terrified "What's wrong?", I said. He starts to tell me he has had the worst day ever. "Oh, what happened?" He tells me he had a bad day at school, and came home, laid down on the couch, and took out his retainer and put it on the coffee table. And Carter the dog ATE his tooth in the retainer. When he told me this, I was so speechless, I couldn't even yell at him.

But, luckily, we are nothing if not a creative family. I made him a fake tooth out of oven baked clay and we superglued it to the retainer. It's a little crooked, but not too bad.

Work Stories: #1. Dot is a tech at Piedmont. She's so sweet, but she left her husband and kids for a woman, when she decided she was gay. Anyway, she ended up living with Rita, one of our nurses (gay) who we had to let go because of suspected drug abuse. So, one day, Dot gets home from work and FEDERAL AGENTS are all over their apartment looking for drugs. Apparently Rita and Judith (her partner) had stolen prescription pads from a lot of hospitals and were getting them filled all over the city. They caught Rita at work in the ER and arrested her! Rita and Judith are now in rehab together and Dot is watching her dogs.

Work Story #2: Cheyenne, one of our techs, actually we call her our "hippie, white trash tech," is married, has an illegitimate child that her mother is raising because Cheyenne used to be on heroin. Then we have this darling physician's assistant, David, who has been dating, May forever. Seems that Cheyenne and David got caught coming out of a bathroom together on night shift, and guess what was going on there? I guess May found out and then David proposed. Stay tuned.

Hayley had this creepy guy, Kevin, who liked her.

And Claire, what a treat! It has been so much fun this year to go to the basketball games and watch her cheer. She has so many friends. She and Kelsey look like twins, and are best friends. A whole group of them have walked to school together for three years, but it wasn't until this year that she and Kelsey realized that they liked each other.

My life—I had a guy I was briefly interested in. Turns out he is Dave's clone where money is concerned==incredibly cheap. Alan took me out to the $1.00 movie (our first date) and brought snacks for us so that we wouldn't have to "waste money" at the snack bar. What did he bring? He gave us each a ½ peanut butter sandwich (he had made) and a GENERIC can of orange juice. I can't go there again. I'd rather live the rest of my life alone than to have to go back to counting every penny.

May 2, 2003 - Claire

Ok, what is Mom's problem? Okay so she is limiting our computer time and taking away DSL. Only because Hayley is on it 24/7. And I'm like "That's not fair. I'm never on it." Why should I have to suffer for what she and Grant did? And then Mom's like "What are you, the Drama Queen, tonight?" I just went to my room. Just a second ago. She opens the door "Is Ginger in here?" I'm like "No." Then she slams the door. And I'm like "Thanks." This morning at 8:10, she is like "I think Ginger needs to go potty, will you take her out?" And there isn't a question of "Will you," it's actually "Like do it now." And I'm like "Mom, I have to go to school, Kelsey is like here." She wasn't, but I had a little time. When I brought the dogs back in and she thanked me. And I go "Don't thank me, you try this guilt trick with me and expect me to be nice?" She says, "It wasn't that hard." She is a bitch who only cares about herself, uses other people to do stuff and is really annoying.

May 3, 2003 - Margy

Grant's graduation was so exciting. We had sixty people and we were all so happy for him. The only downside was that I had been trying to get my floors refinished for three months, and of course, they weren't done. So everyone had to step over the undone floors in the dining room in order to get any drinks. I guess it wouldn't be my party if everything went as planned. Still, Grant was so excited and I was so happy that my first child had graduated from high school!

Dad, Mom, me, my sister Cindy and her husband, Paul, my brother, Chuck. Claire, Grant and Hayley at Grant's graduation

June 1, 2003 - Claire

So much has happened since last time I wrote. Ok. We had our picnic and then the next day I went to a pool party. There, I met Bryan. He poked me in a tube in the pool and gave me a piggy back ride and swung me. He stopped swinging me and held onto my waist for like 3 minutes. So, the next week was the last week of school And I called him every night and talked to him. On field day, he came and sat next to me. I was like awwwww! So this last day came and we talked and he gave me a back rub and on Tuesday, he, Kelsey, and Patrick and I all went to the movies. And Bryan was annoying me and I knew he was doing it on purpose. LOL.

And the next day, I talked to Patrick online. Patrick: "Do you like Bryan?" Claire: "Maybe."Patrick: "Just tell me." Claire: "Maybe."Patrick: "Ok, that's yes, because you would have said no already." Claire: "Yeah, you're right." Patrick: "Cause he likes you. A lot."Claire: "Really? Is he going to ask me out?"Patrick: "Yeah, I just got off the phone with him." Claire: "Cool." Patrick "You do like him?" Claire: "He's really nice."

That was Wednesday and I thought he might ask me out then but he waited, so at the party, Lisa says, "We were all over each other." So, at 9:30, Bryan took me aside. "Will you go out with me?" And I said, "Seriously?" Because you know, he was laughing and I didn't know.

And he goes "Yes." So, then I say "Oh, yes." And he was like "I'm such a wuss." And I'm like "You?" and he's like "Cause I've wanted to ask you out since Anna's party." And I was like "awwww…..hug." We took pictures and stuff and he gave me his towel and wrapped me up in it. And everyone said that was sooooo cute! So today, we went to the movies. Our first "Official Date" and we like leaned into each other. Then I really had to pee, so I left and then came back and he like put up the armrest and goes "Can I put my arm around you?" And I was like "YEAH!" I had been waiting for him to do that all through the movie! So he put his arm around me and I leaned on him! And it was cute and he like moved his hand down so it was on my hand, then like he was resting on my skirt. It was cute. But, of course that was at the end. And then, while we were walking out, we held hands and stuff. And his sister came up and hugged him. It was fun being under his arm. I felt safe and liked holding hands. That was fun, too. We'll probably do something else soon, like this week.

♥ I ♥ Bryan!

Now, on to family issues. Hayley is obsessed with Kevin. He's mean to her and rude and suicidal! And she like worries about it. And, it's just sick because, she totally buys into it and he ignores her for days and she still likes him. Also, she stays up at night talking on the computer with him.

Mom---really hates that I'm dating and she keeps reminding me that I'm only allowed to "group date." She asks me about Bryan and like I answer, but I know she's just nosy and that annoys me to death. Especially because, like she's the nosiest person I know and I just know she tells her friends. But it annoys the Hell out of me!! Also, she's like obsessed with togetherness. "Let's all sit in the den together because we haven't been together since Friday." And she's always saying stuff like that, over and over. Oh yeah, and Hayley has been making midnight trips to the computer. Which she just got caught at. And deserves it! It's not worth it, to break rules. You are going to get caught. No matter what!

I've known about this for awhile just, I never tell.

Oh yeah, on Field Day, it rained, so we were inside and it was really boring. And like Lizzie hung around Bryan all day, so I thought he liked her, but he left her to sit next to me! LOL

Next person: <u>Grant</u>--Likes a girl, but she stood him up today for a date or was "sick" mysteriously. He's fine, though.

Ok, so that's pretty much it, except my summer list is looking pretty good.

Summer checklist

Friends	X
Hanging out	X
Boyfriend	X
Body	X
Stuff to do	X
Tan(no way)	
Vacations (not very)	
Fun	X (oh, yeah!)

When Bryan asked me out and Mom was taking me home, this was said:

Claire: "Bryan asked me out." Mom: "When?" Claire: "Tonight." Mom:" No, I mean, when are you going out?" Claire:"Now." Mom: "So, did he just say, "Will you go out with me today?'" Claire: "No, he said, "Will you go out with me?'" Mom: "Oh. (times have changed, Mom!) He seems nice (let's just say that was hard for her to get out)

I ♥ Bryan

Love ya,

Claire

June 3, 2003 - Claire

Hey, it's been a long day. Like really long. It stared at 8:30, when I went babysitting for four kids. Only me! And let's face it, one of me, four of them, that's a lot. Erica called and I never called her back. LOL! Oh, well. I babysat until 4:15!! And I got $80. Ok, like I talk to Bryan twice a day. And he wants to see me this week. And the only day I can do is Sunday. He's like "Why does your Mom want togetherness? Can't I come and steal you away?" It was like awwwww! Also, I was saying some person on "Smallville" couldn't be a teacher because she was too pretty and Bryan was like "I guess you can't be one." And it took me awhile and I was like "awwww, that's sweet." Mom's been like weird. She tries to connect with me. I know she's not comfortable with me having a boyfriend. It's really annoying and it feels like we aren't really connecting. I just want to say "Mom, I know you are uncomfortable with me dating Bryan, but you are going to have to ACCEPT IT. And he really likes me and I really like him, so you are just going to have to accept that.

I'm really tired. 4 Kids!! ALL DAY LONG! Anyways, I have been like so busy, no time for family, friends, boyfriend, and like I really want to do stuff with them. I should go.

I ♥Bryan
♥ Ya
Claire

June 4, 2003 - Claire

Ok, so today I went to the movies with Bryan, Kelsey, Ali, Chris, Freddy, Patrick and Abby. Anyway, at dinner, Mom asked, "So, you and Bryan haven't had your first fight yet?" What kind of statement is that? It's my business, not hers and I will tell her when I want to. I hate it when she butts into my business like that. And I don't tell her anything because I don't trust her with it. And I don't want her to know. She obviously is too old school for me, if you catch my drift.

At the movies, like through more than half the movie, Bryan and I didn't make contact. Then he moved and I was like "What are you doing?" and he's like "I was going to put my arm around you." And I was like "Go ahead!" So, he did and I leaned on him and he had his hand around mine and then it was touching my skirt and like he would move his hand and it went up my leg! And we just cuddled, it was great! But I was like thinking. good thing I shaved! And put lotion on! LOL So, then I hung out at Kelsey's house until 11:30 and I went upstairs and didn't say "Hi" because Hayley told me Mom was really mad. So Mom comes up here. "Why didn't you say hi? Are you just not saying it now?" I was like "No, but I was tired, and I just came upstairs." She goes "Well next time at least say 'Hi' so I know you're home." And then she goes into it about the dogs and how Ginger always gets out. Ok, whatever. "You should take this seriously." I'm like "Okay." She is obsessed with Ginger. The brattiest ugliest, most annoying and stupidest dog ever. So then Mom comes in again and goes 'I'm sorry, just say 'hi' next time, ok?" I'm like "Ok, ok." But with the Bryan thing and I feel so safe in his arms and it's real. I love it. He's a good boyfriend, at least. I think he is good enough for me. Love ya,

I ♥ Bryan,
Claire

June 5, 2003 - Claire

Mom, she came home and said "Ok, I figured out what is bothering me." Claire: "Ok." Mom: "You never have your friends over here, you always go over there" Claire: "Well, it's easier." Mom: "Look, if you have your friends over once a week, that would be enough." Claire: "Ok." (like totally confused. She always said no friends over when she wasn't home.) Mom "Well, when I wasn't working YESTERDAY you could have come over here." Claire: "Ok, but we like it at Kelsey's." Mom: "Well it would be nice to have your friends over here." (a guilt trip)

Then later, she says "No, you can't sleep over at Kelsey's because I'm working four days this week and you need to be home earlier." I'm so SICK OF HER BEHAVIOR. She's like a little kid!!! I hate it to Death!! Anyway, I talked to Bryan.

I ♥ Bryan

♥ ya, Claire

June 8, 2003 - Claire

Thank God! Mom has cooled down a bit, but still is edgy, which isn't too good, but better. I called Jennifer and she said; "You look like you lost a lot of weight and your stomach has sunken in. You know the day at Silver Ridge, you looked really thin." I said, "You know I lost like 10 pounds, but I needed to lose it." And I wouldn't be anorexic. I couldn't, it's not possible. I just like jogging and like I have been eating less. I still eat a ton. I'm serious. I eat all the time and when I feel like it.

Anyway, the Bryan news. I found out from Jennifer, that Stephanie K. DUMPED him!! And that shocked me. A LOT! That's why one day he said he punched his punching bag and broke his knuckle and didn't want to talk about it. I can't believe she dumped him. Who would dump Bryan? I know I won't. Today I went to his pool and hung out with him and his family and Bryan's little sister did not like me at all. I don't think Shannon, his older sister, did either, but a little more than the little sister. I can tell Bryan really likes me. It's really sweet. Like on the phone he said, "The highlight of my day was hanging out with you." I was like awwwww! That's cute! And he calls me twice a day! I really like him so that's cool. We will probably be together for a long time. Oh, yeah, and when I told him that Jennifer thought I looked anorexic, he was like "You look fine. I like the way you look. You look fine, not anorexic, you're always eating!" (He laughed)

Anyway, Dad is going to take me to Las Vegas. We're staying with his friend who has a kid close to my age! Kool, huh? But I'm happy with Bryan! Really happy!! Dad even said Bryan could go to Six Flags with us. Kool, huh? So we will go at the end of June. Fun fun. I also love his eyes. They are like so pretty. I could look into them forever.

I ♥ BryanClaire

June 10, 2003 - Claire

Today I went to Bryan's house. And you know, hung out. There is a problem, I don't talk at all around his family. I guess they kind of scare me or something. I just shut my mouth and don't say anything. I don't know why I do this, either. I guess when I'm uncomfortable, I do that. But I never have done that before, only when I was younger. Bryan can tell that I am uncomfortable.He even asked me about it and I was like "I don't know why. I just don't talk around them." I even tried, but I couldn't bring myself to do it. I had thought maybe he's getting sick of me. What if he breaks up with me? OMG. I don't know what I would do. I can't imagine. But he really didn't like that I didn't talk very much to his family. It just scared me. You know, being around all those people and not knowing what to do and being scared of making a bad impression. Feeling like you are being judged on everything. And I guess I'm overprotective of Bryan, a little. But I mean, who really wants another girl to sit on her boyfriend? But, Bryan did put me in his lap and hold me there. He pretty much had his hand on my boobs when we were lying down. But like my hand was under it and I moved it down my stomach. In the pool, before he saw me around his family (key phrase), he kept holding me and stuff. The bad thing about being in a relationship is that you don't know when they are annoyed with you or want you to act differently or are going to break up with you. I think Bryan is going to break up with me. I hope not, but, like I said, you never know. But he is definitely sick of me because when he left he was like "I might call you." That's not an "I'll call you." That's an "I'll call you if I feel like it and if I don't feel like it, then I won't." And luckily, our phone line isn't working, so I won't be able to talk for awhile. I really hope he isn't going to break up with me.

I ♥ Bryan
♥ Claire

June 12, 2003 - Claire

Ok, yesterday we got back from a week at Hilton Head and on that trip, I was mature, no outbursts or anything. Amelia and Hayley are way too sarcastic and it annoys the Hell out of me. And let's face it, Keeley and I aren't both interested in boys because I am, but she isn't, so it's hard to meet people. I got so sick of my family, like you know I can't stand them at home for like 2 days, so you can imagine a week? And we got back and like I was talking to Bryan and ACCIDENTALLY said "Prince William is cute" (something like that) and he FLIPPED out. And I was like "What the heck?" All I did was say he was cute. I didn't say I wanted to get together with him or anything. And I'm like "Is there anything I can do to make you feel better?" He's like "No." So, you know what's the point of me keeping apologizing. I was like, forgive, forget and move on. So today he just pretended like it didn't happen. He's gotten more courage to do things with me, THANK GOD! Luv ya,
Claire
I ♥ Bryan

July 6, 2003 - Claire

So now I am into July, not knowing what is happening. And I am going to be in my cousin, Stephanie's wedding, Kool!

August 29, 2003 - Claire.

Tomorrow we go to camp at 3am. Ok, so I was talking to Bryan and he says, "You are conceded." And what was I supposed to say "No!" and then he would have argued with me. So I was like "Ok, I guess." He's like "Yeah, you know when I said it's surprising you have never have gone out with anyone else before except for that guy and then you were like I know!" What am I supposed to say to that? I guess I am conceded. But, like you know I wish he didn't tell me that. Also the other guy I went out with doesn't exist. I made him up to sound like I had actually gone out with someone. So, like yeah, I don't want to lie and say "Oh, I went out with him," but I didn't. I'm like afraid, if we break up, he will tell people. Which I don't want people knowing at all. This has been one of my most guarded secrets ever. I'm going to bed. Have to wake up at 3:00am. LOL
Cya,
Claire
I ♥ Bryan

July 27-28, 2003 - Claire

Camp was awful. I had an awful time. All I could do was hang out with Michelle and Alicia, who are like best friends and, ok, let's face it; I'm not as good a friend to them. I'm kind of left out and it's not too much fun. Michelle is the whiner, seriously she whines like it's nobody's business. It's annoying, and then the rest of the squad ignores us. It's not too cool, and like I tried, but they really ignore us. Anyway, on the Bryan front. I don't know why, but he hasn't kissed me yet. I'm really starting to think he doesn't want to. Or like I'm disgusting or ugly or something. It has been 2 f**king months! Most people have kissed by one month! And I think he hates when I repeat stories or talk about nothing, because he doesn't care, but you know what? I'm sick of starting the conversations. It's not fair. I am always the one doing it. I'm the energy in this relationship. I called him first, invited him places, and it took him two weeks to ask me out, which, by then, I didn't even think he was going to. And now I want to give him credit for something, but I'm getting really sick of waiting. It's stressing me out and it shouldn't be. Maybe one of these days, I'll do it instead of waiting for him!! Also, I hate feeling like he's more popular than me. It just feels that way, all the time. I absolutely don't like Shannon, his sister. She is snotty, self centered and bitchy. And the favorite of the family, which gets to me. I really don't like her. I also said "I love you" first, which currently, I don't think I mean it, but I know later, I will. Cya,Claire

July 28, 2003 - Claire

Hey, today was mini camp and then the banquet and then, surprise! A trip to the movies. Ok, the movie is definitely the most interesting. We waited around for like an hour for the movie to start. In which, I managed to fart in front on Bryan. Really, really embarrassing. So, we are in the movies and Bryan puts his hand on my leg. He starts at one end of my leg and goes to my butt. Right. Yes, under the skin and thank God, not under the underwear. Then it would have been too much but like he moved and said "weise", and then moved again and was like I'm not even going to say. I was like yeah, I have an idea. DUH! It was a boner. Then, we were in the car and I was sitting on him. I could like feel it moving and let's just say it wasn't his leg. Like all the while he had his hand like up my skirt. I was wondering what he was doing and if it was like, you know, OK. So I realized what the reason was today at Blockbuster. This guy and a friend came up to me and said "Can I have a hug?" and I said "Sure." Making sure my you-know- what's didn't touch him. Then he made small talk and slapped my butt so I moved away. "I have a boyfriend," I said. And he goes "Well, I'm sure he would want me to do this," and he grabs my butt and I move away and then he puts his arm around me and I moved away and slapped him. (hard)

Back to the movie, I think Bryan was like trying

to prove he can do stuff like this with me because I am his girlfriend. WRONG!.

Love Ya,
Claire
I ♥ Bryan

July 28, 2003

Summer is going by way too fast. We had a great time at Hilton Head. It's so odd to see the younger girls (Claire and Keeley) not needing us to supervise them all the time. Claire has a boyfriend. Bryan. He's so cute and seems to really like her. He calls her all the time, which will probably get old with her. But they are so cute together and we're going through the drama of when he will kiss her, etc. etc. We were at the cheerleading banquet a couple of weeks ago. Bryan was there because his mother, Tammy, is a cheerleading coach, and coached Claire in eighth grade. Bryan sat with Claire and asked her to go to the movies afterwards, with his sister. It was so cute, my baby on a date! Of course, this has opened a whole new can of worms about dating that I didn't have to deal with for Grant and Hayley.

It's funny to see a child of mine a cheerleader. Or to go to these meetings, where all these beautiful, perfect mothers are, with their perfect marriages and perfect children. And there am I, with my ratty clothes, my hair never perfect, divorced. It's like they're a different species from me. When I was in high school, I was always the bookish, didn't fit in type. Claire just fits in with these kids without a problem. She's so lucky.

July 29, 2003 - Claire

I'm like soooo....tired. Mini camp, tumbling , dinner, errands, home. It was long and you know what ...all I could think about was Bryan. Was my butt hairy? Did he notice when I farted? Did he get offended when I didn't say 'excuse me?' Did he notice how many times I have done that, did he think my butt was small? Did he think I

thought it was ok that he could just sit there with his hand up my skirt and be holding my ass? All this has been running through my head all day. It is sooooo......annoying. I'm going to bed.
Good night!

July 30, 2003 - Claire

OMG! I just had my first kiss!! Well, ok. We like kissed on the couch but that doesn't count. Bryan tried to French me and I like did for a minute, but put my head down. I was like sooooo bad. It was embarrassing. I'm really bad. I need to practice now. I'm hyped, but really tired and I can't believe how weird that was. Bryan, at the cheerleading banquet, was flirting with another girl and he asked me for her name. I said "No." And he goes "Why not?" I said: "You liked her." He said: "No, I didn't."I ♥ Bryan.

August 10, 2003 - Margy

The first day of school is tomorrow. Tonight, Claire is on my bed sobbing her heart out because she has to break up with Bryan. She doesn't love him anymore. Hayley and I are standing there, dumbfounded, not knowing what to say. Finally, I tell Claire not to rush it, give him a chance. I don't know why she feels like she has to break up with him, and she can't or won't tell me.

Seeing her sobbing and thinking that school is starting tomorrow, gives me a bad feeling. Usually, the night before school starts is always so exciting, but all I can think is I hope this isn't a bad omen for the school year.

August 12, 2003 - Claire

Second day of school. Have to update. At the lock- in, Kelsey and I met 3 guys, twins and their friend. Joe was the friend. We had an awesome time hanging out. Feel guilty about Bryan. Go to cookout, see cute, tall boys. Went to a football game and couldn't believe my boyfriend had a rainbow-colored face. First day of school, bad. Got nervous, hard classes. Cheerleading sucked. I couldn't lift Kimmy in extension. Not doing so good in cheerleading. Talked to Joe. Today was better. Although at the assembly, Jared like held my hand in front of Bryan and I am sure Bryan was like flipping out inside. I am giving it a week with Bryan. Tonight he did not call me. Which I think is kind of weird because he always does. We're going to break up soon. At the lock-in, Stephanie and Madison were spying on me. I hope they didn't call Bryan and tell him. Oh, I bet they did because I am getting the feeling that they did. I get the feeling I know they did. Ok, night now. Can't sleep

Claire's 9th grade cheerleading picture

August 19, 2003 - Claire

I have broken up with Bryan. On Saturday and on the phone. Here is our conversation:

Claire: "Hi Bryan." Bryan: "Hey." Claire: "Where are you?" Bryan: "Hanging with Shannon's friends." Claire: "Oh, Ok. Look I think it would be better if we're just friends because I am so busy right now with cheerleading and school, I think you need someone with more time."Bryan: "Yeah, I understand." Claire: "Bye." (hang up)

Ok, so I went to the movies on Sunday and saw Shannon's friend there and she said Shannon said he was fine.

Monday, I go to school and Bryan can't even look at me. He won't even speak to me or at least say "Hi." Today he said "hi," which was big step up. And like we were talking to Chris on the way home and he said that Bryan thinks I'm the biggest bitch ever because I had everything and I just let it all go. Which isn't true. So yeah, now, today I saw Bryan in the hall, flirting with other girls, so I'm glad he got over it.

G2G

I ♥ Joe!

Claire.

August 24, 2003 - Claire

It's my half birthday. We went to Asphalt yesterday and it was great and Joe was there and we had fun. I really like Joe. I want to go out with him, but he told me that he was going to wait for a little bit and then do it. I'm totally cool with that, but I really, really, really like him. And I love hugging him because I reach his shoulders and it's really kool. I mean I'm short. I can't wait until we go out, though. Maybe we will go to Homecoming together. I just love it because I love hugging him and he is sooo nice and sweet and funny and kind. Ok, I know but he is so kool. I can't wait for 2 weeks, to see him, but I will because I am just that strong. Anyway, I'm exhausted. We had a car wash on Saturday and Carly "the slut" and her followers were there. Ben was fingering her at lunch. They have been going out for a week. I was just remembering when Bryan had his hand on my ass and how much I didn't like that. I'm glad I'm through with him. G2G, Love ya.

I ♥ Joe

Claire

September 1, 2003 - Claire

Ok, so Joe said he was going to call and for like a week he didn't and I, of course, freaked out and got mad. I mean he says he's going to call and doesn't. I don't know why either. So, I talk to him and he doesn't like it when I freak out when he doesn't call so I told him I wouldn't anymore. I don't know if he likes me anymore. I hope he does because I like him. But I won't call him this week at all and I won't get mad if he doesn't call. I just hope I didn't ruin it for us, I really like him. I want to talk to him

sometime this week to see if he still feels the same way. I pray that I didn't ruin it.

♥ ya,

Claire

September 21, 2003 - Claire

We had a debate tournament on Friday and Saturday. I got 4 hours of sleep between both days. Ok. Carly won 5-0. She never does any work at all. Her partner does it all. Which is very obvious.

I don't like Joe. He's kind of gayish. Anyway, on Friday night, the Varsity Group stayed out all night. They drank and smoked and flashed the Air Force guys for a kick. I thought this was really bad role model action. I'm embarrassed that Hayley was involved in this. On the bus ride home, no one saved me and Evelyn a seat, so we were trying to sit in the back. I was like trying to sit with Gary and Ovais and they were like "No" and Matt goes "Dude, she has a Great Ass and she's about to shove it in your face." And he was like "Yeah." And then Mrs. Jolly (bitch) made me move so I like couldn't get by so I like wiggled it in his face. I was 100% complimented that I had a Great Ass.

So, since I have gotten back, Mom has been all clingy. Like "Oh, do you want to come watch this with me?" And then she'll come upstairs with me and try to talk to me about some book which I don't care about. And she tries to get me involved in Hayley's life. As a good influence. And I'm not going to get in the middle of her business. I shouldn't be forced to. Mom was also trying to get me to communicate with Bryan. And I refused.

Mom's like "You want to go see the movie "Cold Mountain" with me tomorrow?"

C---"No, I have homework." M---"Well, it's only 2 and a half hours out of your day." C---"Whatever." (I'm sick of her).

September 30, 2003 - Margy

This is the worst thing. I knew I had a bad feeling about this year. Hayley and the whole debate team got in trouble on a debate tournament. Turns out, instead of staying in their rooms after curfew, one of the ninth grade girls left her room, met an army guy and he gave her a beer, which she shared with all of the girls in the room. I have had to see the principal and Mr. Stevens, her debate coach. He is devastated. He loves these kids as much as we do. I don't know if they will be suspended or kicked off the team. I am just so upset that Hayley did that. What was she thinking?

Work has been crazy. Mary Beth, the coordinator quit and I am now "acting coordinator" for the ED. Out of nursing for fifteen years, only back in four years, and I'm a coordinator. I don't know if that means that I'm good, or nursing is desperate. Probably a little bit of both. Still, it's exciting to run the whole ED, and I try to be fair and honest with people. Actually, I'm pretty well liked from Joella, the cleaning lady (and my friend) on up.

October 6, 2003 - Margy

Well, Hayley and the other six kids involved will have to go to drug and alcohol classes. Four classes, twice a week for two weeks. I am so embarrassed. I had to go to Cindy, the timekeeper, to help me rearrange my schedule. And I had to tell her why. She is very sweet.

The funny story in all this is Claire was on the same trip. On the following Monday, one of the kids involved said "Well, what did you do Friday night?" Claire said "Well, I stayed in my room." The kid said "Boy, are you boring." Claire said she thought to herself 'I may be boring, but I'm not expelled from school.'

November 4, 2003 - Margy

Hayley and Claire are sister debaters (first time in Chattahoochee history) They are so close, it's special to see. Sometimes they have sleepovers in Hayley's room and talk about their mutual friends.

Well, things have settled down since the debate team debacle. Claire has been saying that she wants to drop out of cheerleading, she doesn't like it anymore, she wants to concentrate on debate. I'm not sure what that is about. She had wanted to be and enjoyed being a cheerleader. She is just so busy, I'm not sure if she knows what she wants. I told her she needs to finish this semester and then we'll decide. By then, cheerleading will be over anyway, and she can focus on debate and see if that's what she wants.Sometimes Claire seems moodier, or more dramatic than usual, but she has so much on her plate. And when she gets stressed, her headaches start coming back.

I have loved going to her football games, and I hate football. Dave comes, too, and we pretend we don't see each other. I just feel so proud watching her out there doing the cheers. She is one of the four that can do the back handspring and she's working on her tuck. It's so neat! For Christmas, my parents are taking the whole family on a cruise. How cool is that? Kids are really excited—can't wait.

Work is going really well. I'm a coordinator and I get to help people on so many levels. First, the patients--I get them back as soon as I can so they don't have to wait. Then, the staff and doctors. They come to me with their complaints and problems and I get to troubleshoot and come up with ideas. It's a rewarding job and I get to know EVERYTHING---which of course, I love. Nursing has changed so much since I first went into it. And I'm glad. I mean when I started, if I was charting and a doctor came up to me, I would have to stand up and give him my chair. Now, the doctor will ask us where a patient is, and ask us where he should sit. Go figure!

November 22, 2003 - Claire

I had a competition today!! We got third in JV, as freshmen. We were the only freshman squad!!! It's great. I'm so excited. We had to get up at 5:00am!! After I got home, Hayley and I decided to go to the movies. We just didn't want Mom to come. She is so annoying. I want her to shut up sometimes. Especially last week, she kept asking me if I knew where the competition was. Like about 3 times a day she would ask me. And then follow up questions "Do you know what time you're competing?" "Do you know when varsity is?" If I don't know where it is, how am I going to know the times!!! So Hayley and I went to the movies, and guess who I saw there? Bryan and Patrick, my favorite people. I, of course, pretended they weren't there. Of course, Bryan had a hickey. I mean his girlfriend is a slut. MAJOR. I'm glad we broke up!!! ☺

Back to Mom. So Hayley and I decided to watch "Old School" at home. It's rated R for a reason. So Mom decided to watch it with us and the second scene is the wife watching porn and so I tell Mom "Hey, Mom, Me and Hayley just want to watch this movie." So you know, she will leave. She obviously isn't going to approve either way. She leaves. And now, she's mad at me for kicking her out. I DON'T GIVE A SHIT!! I don't have to watch every movie with her. Maybe I don't want her to watch a movie with me. Who cares!! She's so obsessive and weird.

December 12, 2003 - Claire

OMG! Mom needs to have a reality check!! She keeps trying to give all these guilt trips. Like, on the cruise, she says, "You'll hang out with me, right?" ("No!") "Remember, I have the money!!" (No one cares). And then last weekend was Ohio Valley Debate and she's like "I know you would have rather hung out with your friends (Hell, yeah) but I enjoyed hanging out with you. (I f**king didn't). An entire weekend with my Mom! How lame!! I hate guilt trips! I'm never guilty because I don't care! Oh yeah and like yesterday, I was sitting around and she says, "Go clean your room" (I ignore her) "Or else you're grounded." She can't ground me. I'm going on a cruise!! And another time she tells me to put my shoes away, and I wanted to finish my homework and then do it. And she starts yelling at me about being lazy. And I go "I don't care!" Mom: "Do you need to go to bed early?" (Honestly I wouldn't mind going to bed early) But going to bed early is not a punishment and wow, I deserved punishment for that. I used some seriously harsh language!!Donna likes to think she is so slutty, but honestly isn't, and that seriously annoys me! Oh yeah, Mom again. I was on the computer and she's like "What are you doing?" "Why?" and she came by later and asks the exact same things. She was wasting my time and I don't want to talk to her. She also wants to know everything about me. I'm not telling her stuff. She's so annoying and no one likes her. I'm tired as Hell.

  Claire

December 22, 2003 - Margy

I didn't know that you could be cold on cruise ships, but apparently we got the first one in five years where the weather is down in the 40's. This would be okay had we known to have brought warm clothes. However, when all you pack are shorts and T shirts, this is a bit of a problem.

Other than that, we had a great time. So much to do and see. Every night the family gets together for dinner, but the rest of the time we're on our own. Grant, Hayley and Claire each found a group their own age and are having a great time. To be perfectly honest, it's a little boring for me, It's hard to be single on a cruise ship, where it's all couples and family. But still, nice to relax.

Yesterday, it was so cold that Hayley, Claire and I were lying in our bunks, wrapped up and trying to keep warm. We were talking and started giggling about something and we couldn't stop. We must have gone on for like fifteen minutes. I thought to myself "Oh God, thank you so much for giving me these two perfect girls. Please let us always be this close and don't let anything bad happen to either one of them."

December 28, 2003 - Margy

Well, our usual drama. We hit American soil and I have all these phone messages. I call Jamie, whose son Jordan is watching the dogs, but she's not at home. I call Sandy (who knows everything) and she says "I can't tell you what's going on, talk to Jamie." " We're driving back from Florida, won't be home until six on Christmas Day, so please tell me what is going on." Finally, Sandy tells me. It turns out that the first time Jordan let the dogs out, my beloved Ginger escapes, and no one has seen her since. We are all so upset, Claire is crying. We have had the greatest trip, and now we have had the worst news. The drive home takes forever.

We get home and the kids and I all go in different directions, looking for Ginger. No luck. Dave is supposed to pick the kids up to take them skiing for the next week. Hayley has a bad cold and says she's too sick to go.

I talk to Shelley, my eternal optimist. She says not to give up on Ginger, remember she found her dog, Melanie, after 2 days. Of course, Melanie weighs thirty pounds, not six pounds. She starts looking for Ginger in her neighborhood, and puts out a "Ginger Alert". The next day, December 26, I go to Kinko's and print $30 worth of posters with a big color picture of Ginger on it. I hang them on every phone pole I can find in a two mile radius. I can only pray that someone has found her. I get several phone calls. Ginger has been seen at Chattahoochee High School, on Jones Bridge Rd, on Abbott's Bridge Rd. On December 27, as I am finishing a shower, the phone rings. This woman says that she has just seen Ginger running up and down Abbott's Bridge Rd. I say "Are you sure? Because I was there last night, and I didn't see her." She says, yes, she is sure that it's Ginger. I get in the car with wet hair and no shoes and drive to Abbott's Bridge Rd. There, running along the side of the road, is Ginger. I stop the car and get out, and start to walk to her. Ginger looks at me and starts to panic and run across the road. I think "No, God, you can't have gotten me to this point and have me watch my dog get hit!" I bend down and go "Ginger, it's me, Mommy, Ginger, come here." I see, out of the corner of my eye, a car coming down the road, but I can tell that they can see what's going on, and they slow down. At this point, I realize that we're going to be okay. As Ginger hears my voice, it's like a light goes on in her eyes, and they get large. She rushes up to me and starts kissing my face. She is HOME! I drive home with her and go into Hayley's bedroom (where she is still sleeping). Tink, Carter and Ginger have a great reunion, on Hayley's bed, and she wakes her up. I call Ginger "my Christmas miracle." I cannot believe that after eight days, in 30-degree weather, we have found this six pound dog alive! I am so grateful. It is a miracle. But I keep thinking, I hope I haven't used my miracle on a dog. I hope I won't need a miracle for something else, and not have it because I've already used it. But what else could I need it for?

December 31, 2003 - Margy

Another year is over. What a way to go out with the cruise and dog and all. Wonder what the New Year will hold? Claire has been having more headaches, so I made an appointment with her to see Dr. Springer on January 3rd. She also had some wild story about how she couldn't ski because she had frostbite or something, which she doesn't have. I hope 2004 is even better than 2003.

January 9, 2004 - Margy

Dr. Springer said he thought that Claire was having "cluster migraines" and we just needed to break them up. She is no better, perhaps even worse. Says she feels terrible and is starting to miss school. She says she has headaches all the time and feels bad. Dr. Springer switches her to another medicine and says "Let's just order a Cat Scan to rule out anything else." It's scheduled for January 14th.

On the odd side, Ginger has started to sleep with her body wrapped around Claire's head. This is weird on two levels: Claire and Ginger have never liked each other; and Ginger has always slept with me, under my arm. Another odd thing, Claire has started sleeping with me because of she doesn't feel well, and her sleep has become very restless, she mumbles and sometimes will sit up and open her eyes. It's kind of scary.

January 13, 2004 - Margy

For dinner tonight, I made spaghetti. It was really good. When I was in bed and unable to sleep around midnight, I kept thinking about that spaghetti. Finally, I get up, heat up the spaghetti and am eating it. It's delicious. About halfway into it, Claire comes down and tells me she thinks she's anorexic. That's why she can't eat. Talk about an appetite suppressant. I kept looking at this spaghetti and then her. I don't finish it.

January 14, 2004 - Margy

Well, we had the Cat Scan and they called and said that they needed to do an MRI because it looked like an enlarged blood vessel or something; nothing to worry about. It's scheduled for Friday, January 16th. Oh well, I guess on Friday while I wait for her in the MRI, I'll call around to find eating disorder specialists. I hate it when my kids are sick.

Friday, January 16, 2004 2:00 a.m. - Margy

Claire has a **Brain Tumor**. I found out today when I called Dr. Springer's office to get the results of Claire's MRI.

Dr. Springer comes right on the phone and says, "I'm glad you called." He is clearly upset about something. I wonder what's going on, and then it hits me: he has some bad news for me! He says quickly, "I just got Claire's MRI results and it shows she has a brain tumor." There is silence on the line. Finally, I say, "A brain tumor?" It feels like the room has moved, and I look down at my feet to make sure they are still on the floor. They are.

Dr. Springer goes on to say that he is trying to get Claire in to see a neurosurgeon as soon as possible, and then he puts me on hold to check on the appointment. I stand in the kitchen, clutching the phone, in shock. I can't move. Dr. Springer comes back on the line and says his office will have to call me back about the appointment; they are still working on it. I ask, "What kind of brain tumor do they think it is?" Dr Springer says, "They aren't sure, but they think it might be a glioma."

I get off the phone and just stand there, with the phone still in my hand. As a nurse, I know that I'm in shock, but I'm in such shock, I don't know what to do. Grant must have heard part of my conversation, or the way my voice changes, because he comes in the kitchen and says in his loud, irritating voice, "WHAT?" I say, "Claire has a brain tumor." His eyes get huge, he has a look of horror on his face, tears start to fall down his cheeks and my autistic son, who HATES to be touched, walks over and awkwardly hugs me.

Dr. Springer's office calls back and says we have an appointment with a Dr. Hudgens, a neurosurgeon, on Tuesday at 4:00 p.m. I start to say, "I have to work that day…" but I say nothing, and write down the information. Work doesn't matter anymore.

I hang up the phone and it rings again - it's Dave. Dave never calls during the day, and he starts out asking for Grant. I blurt out to him "Dave, Dr. Springer's office just called and Claire has a brain tumor. They say it might be a glioma. Please tell me she'll be ok." In that second before he responds, for the first time in six years, I know exactly how Dave feels. His heart has split in two, just like mine. After being divorced all this time, I know what he's feeling again.

Hayley is out of town on a debate trip. Should I tell her or wait till she gets home? She has been as worried about Claire as the rest of us. But, maybe she'll be so caught up in her trip that she'll forget to ask. I decide I'll handle this when I talk to her.

Finally, I go upstairs to tell Claire. The shades are drawn, and the room is dark, even though it's the middle of the day. It's so odd to see Claire lying in bed during the day. I have trouble getting her to go to bed at night. Claire opens her eyes when I enter the room. I sit on the bed; I want to appear calm, controlled. I take a deep breath and feel this incredible nausea wash over me. I swallow hard, take another deep breath and say "Claire, Dr. Springer's office called. Your MRI shows that you have a brain tumor, which is why you haven't been feeling well." I can tell by the look in her eyes that she's not sure what I'm talking about. So I say, "There's a spot in your brain that isn't working right, and it's making you sick; you don't have anorexia. The spot is causing you to feel bad. But Dr. Springer is going to get another doctor to look at your MRI and we'll figure out what to do about it. You are going to be ok." I feel another wave of nausea wash over me as I finish talking. To have to tell my child she has a brain tumor. How cruel! Claire nods, and still doesn't say anything. My drama queen is speechless, I'm not sure what she's feeling or understanding. But I don't want to keep going over the tumor; it may make her more scared. So I say, "Do you have any questions?" She shakes her head no and so I say "Because of this, you don't have to go on the debate trip today, if you don't feel well enough to go." She shakes her head and says, "I just want to stay home and sleep." I say, "That's fine. I'll let you sleep. I love you." And I kiss her sweet cheek. As I walk downstairs, it feels like the stairs have tripled in size, it's the longest walk I have ever made in my house.

Hayley calls later tonight. Of course, she asks how Claire's MRI went. I say we aren't sure yet, but Claire isn't going on the debate trip. I can tell by the silence on the line that Hayley is suspicious. Why are kids so smart? I don't think I should tell her that her sister has a brain tumor while she's out of town. I don't want her to freak out and lose it. But I don't know if that's the right thing to do. I no longer know what the right thing to do is.

January 18, 2004 4:30 p.m. - Margy

Claire and I go shopping today, for lack of anything better to do. She wants to shop alone, so I sit at the mall, waiting until it's time for us to meet. I am watching the people walk by. Some people are with others, some people are alone. People are laughing and talking. I get up and walk around. This must be how a schizophrenic feels. I am all alone, and yet all these people are around me, and my body is here, but it isn't interacting with anyone. I look at the store window displays. Everything is so pretty, but I think "The only thing I want in this whole world is my daughter's health." I would give anything if it was a week ago and I had no idea that my beautiful fourteen year old daughter has a brain tumor.

10:30 p.m.

Hayley is home and wants to know about Claire. Claire had told me that she wants to tell Hayley herself, but at the last minute she says, "I can't, Mommy, you tell her." Claire says this as she walks quickly into the living room. As Hayley watches this exchange between Claire and me; Hayley's eyes grow wide with fear. Hayley and I are in the kitchen. "What is going on?" Hayley asks, in that funny, querulous way she has of saying things. I tell Hayley that Claire has a brain tumor. Hayley starts crying and rushes over and hugs me. I hug her back and tell her to go to Claire. She does. I find both of them in the living room, Claire sitting down, Hayley standing over her, hugging Claire. They look so much alike, and yet are so different. Oh please God, don't let us lose her. Please give us hope.

I talk to Dave today. He already has Claire buried. He's talking about "the quality of her life." It's like I see the best in things, and he sees the worst. I don't know if I can do this alone.

Claire is my heart. She is so sweet and cute and delightful. And she deserves to live out her life. I should die first. I volunteer to die first. Take me, not her.

I feel like I'm living a terrible nightmare that I can't wake up from.

Claire is so wonderful, with her high pitched voice and her enthusiasm for life. Please God, give me the strength to be there for her.

Tonight I give her a pain pill because her headache is so bad. For awhile she is ok, but then she freaks out and gets hyperactive and starts running around, and cleaning her room. She keeps yelling at me. Oh God, how can I survive if you take one of my children? Please God, give us all some hope.

<u>My Little Friend</u>
Been there longer than I can remember
No one knows how long
Have you always been there
All along?
I have managed to live with you
All these years
You've never changed
I'm glad for that
When you finally showed your face
We were all shocked
Things got really tough
But you stayed the same
Everyone thought you would hurt me
But, you have always been there
You have always been my little friend
Why would you change now?

By Claire Nelson

Monday, January 19, 2004 2:00 a.m. - Margy

Who knew days could drag so? We're waiting until Tuesday, when we have our appointment with Dr. Hudgen's. As I told Shelley (who is being way too optimistic about this), if he can do surgery to remove the tumor, it's a better prognosis then if he can't. Whoever thought I would pray for brain surgery? I'm not sure who to tell or not tell, but then the more people that know, the more they can pray for Claire. Cindy, my sister, calls about the pictures from the cruise, and I tell her. We decide I'll wait until after Tuesday to tell Mom and Dad. What if it's not as bad as I think it is? That's a laugh. A brain tumor is never good. Last night, as I spend sleepless night number three, lying next to Claire, I reach out and put my hand on her soft cheek. I want to be able to touch her and in doing so, keep her with me forever. I am reminded of when Dave and I were having problems, before our divorce. At night, I would put my hand on his thigh, wishing that by doing this, I could magically keep him beside me, forever. And I knew then that I was losing Dave, just as I know now that I am losing Claire.

Tonight, after the kids have gone to bed, I am sitting in the den, and Claire comes down. She has been crying, her cheeks are all wet. She puts her head in my shoulder and cries and says "Why me, Mommy?" I said, "I don't know. I'm just so sorry." We cry together. Maybe if I had gotten her to the doctor sooner.

Tuesday, January 20, 2004 -Margy

I pick Claire up at school. She is wearing her new plaid skirt, and her $100 Birkenstocks that she had talked me into buying her at the mall (If only she can live long enough to wear them out!). Her hair is in pigtails, and she looks so CUTE, like she's not even sick. All spunky and happy and ready to fight this thing. We meet Dave at Dr. Hudgen's office and go into the examination room. Dr. Hudgen's comes in, introduces himself and puts Claire's MRI films up on the view box. His face is unreadable. He has Claire take some neurological tests. Then he says the worst thing a parent will ever hear. That Claire does have a glioma. Surgery isn't an option for her tumor. Typically, kids between five to ten years get it, so she is a little old to have it show up now. It is fast growing, there is no cure. This tumor is usually malignant, but since they can't biopsy it, they have no way of knowing for sure. With a tumor this fast growing, the only options are radiation and chemo. Even though both ot these options have terrible side effects, this is the only way to extend Claire's life.

Then he calls in his associate, a Dr. Mazewski. She is a neuropediatric oncologist, or something. She walks in, and oddly enough, her name is Claire, too. She says to call her Dr. Claire. She has grayish-blonde hair pulled back with a barrette and big owlish glasses. She reaffirms what Dr. Hudgen's has just said.

As they continue talking, a surreal feeling comes over me and I find myself slipping away. It's like I'm watching this scene from a distance. Dave and I are sitting next to each other on one side of the rather large room. Claire is in the middle, sitting on the exam table. Dr. Hudgens, his assistant, and Dr. Claire are on the other side of the room. I see myself, holding my little tape recorder (which I brought so I can play it back later, in case I forget what they say or recommend.). Halfway through their speech, I watch myself turn it off. I will never forget what they are saying, here, and I will never again play this tape.

As I watch this scene continue to unfold, it's like I'm once again watching the soap operas I used to love. This must be a soap opera! This must be a sound stage that we're on. This can't be happening to us. This just doesn't happen in real life. Any minute, someone will yell "CUT!" '

I come back to my body when I hear Claire say to Dr. Hudgen's "What if I don't get chemo and radiation?" He says, "Then you won't live to see your sixteenth birthday."

Dr. Claire has my Claire do a more extensive neurological exam. Claire can't even walk a straight line, heel to toe. I'm horrified to realize I didn't even know she was this bad. Six weeks ago, she was doing cartwheels. Claire sits alone on the exam table as they talk to us. That even though this isn't a great tumor to get, with a positive attitude and with chemo and radiation, she may still beat it. They are also encouraged because Claire didn't present with the typical symptoms that this tumor usually presents with. Maybe that means it's a slower growing tumor than usual.

Tears stream down Claire's cheeks. She is so brave. I get up and sit next to her on the exam table. I hug her. Dr. Claire says we need to meet with a Dr. Schoenfeld, at Piedmont, to set up radiation tomorrow. And we need to decide what kind of chemo, but there's not as much of a rush on that. Dr. Claire also wants to get another MRI at Scottish Rite Hospital.

After we're done, and Dave and Claire have walked ahead (and can't hear), I wait for Dr. Claire to give me a prescription for stronger pain pills for Claire. I say, "If this was your daughter would you do chemo and radiation?" She stops writing and thinks for a long minute, and says, "Yes, I would. I would give her the best chance I could." I appreciate her candor.

Claire and I talk about it on the way home. Neither of us likes Dr. Claire. But then who could like someone who just told you that your daughter is probably going to die? I tell Claire that she and I are in this together, and if she wants to fight; I'll be right there beside her, fighting all the way. She squeezes my hand.

We get home about 7:30 and Claire calls Kristen and Kelsey to tell them the news. I call my mom, and tell her. My mom starts to say something, and she breaks down and starts sobbing. My mom, the toughest woman I know starts to cry. I have never heard her cry before, not even at my grandmother's or grandfather's funeral (and she loved her parents more than us kids, I think). This only reaffirms for me that this is as bad a situation as I think it is. Mom is going to tell my brother, Chuck, for me. (I just can't talk about it anymore). I walk around aimlessly upstairs. I have a million things to do, but I can't focus. Finally, I decide to clean Grant and Hayley's bathroom. The doorbell rings and it's Kristen. How sweet of her to come over. She hugs Claire and they go in the den to watch "American Idol." The doorbell rings again and it's Fran with Kelsey. Kelsey goes in the den with Claire and Kristen, and Fran and I walk into the dining room. Fran hugs me and says, "She's going to be just FINE. My niece, Becca, has had a brain tumor since she was five years old, and she's twenty one now. Claire will be ok." This is just what I need: HOPE. It makes me feel better. I don't think I'm strong enough to go through this alone.

I think Grant and Hayley are just shell-shocked. Grant is so upset tonight, after we get back from Dr. Hudgens and tell him what we've learned. He gets all nerdy like he is when he doesn't know what he's feeling. Who can blame him? How are you supposed to act when you hear your little sister has cancer? He needs something to do, so I send him over to Dave's to comfort him. I feel sorry for Dave, all alone. At least I have the kids, and this is one time I am GLAD to share Grant with him. When Grant comes back home later, he's calmer, and says "Dad really appreciates that I went over." He says his father is pretty torn up. Who wouldn't be?

Hayley is just quiet when I tell her what Dr. Hudgen's said. Taking it all in, like she does. Then she goes to her room to do homework and call her boyfriend. I don't know how to comfort her. I don't even know how to comfort myself. After all, my children have been through with the divorce, to then pile this on them, it's so unfair. . We all decide we will stay home tomorrow and regroup.

Wednesday, January 21, 2004 - Margy

We wake up late this morning, and as I walk downstairs, I think "Maybe it's not as bad as I think; maybe I am exaggerating the whole thing." I walk into the kitchen, and see there are thirteen messages on the answering machine. Thirteen people have called us since 8:00am am and it's now 11:00am. So much for positive thinking. Everyone has called, even Pastor Dee. I get the kids up and announce "Ok, Claire wants to fight this tumor, and so we're going to fight this thing together. We are a strong family and we aren't going to let a little brain tumor defeat us. Also, we can't fight it by being negative or hopeless, so we need to do something positive for ourselves, so let's go to IHOP for breakfast." Grant and Hayley say "Yeah!" since we never go out for breakfast. I think it helps them to know that I have hope. And I do; I can't get through this without hope. We have the most fun breakfast, just laughing and talking even though Claire doesn't eat much. Still, she laughs a little. I think we probably all need this before our appointment with Dr. Schoenfeld today.

Hayley comes with us to the doctor and Dave meets us there again. Since it's Wednesday, he'll take Claire out to dinner afterwards.

Well, so much for optimism. This appointment isn't as bad as Dr. Hudgens, but it's close. Claire is to start radiation on Friday, and she'll have six weeks of it. She did ok until Dr. Schoenfeld told her she was going to lose some of her hair at the back of her head, and then he mentioned the words "tumor and "cancer" together. I don't think Claire realized we were saying that her tumor could be cancer. How much bad news should someone have to absorb in a week?

Hayley and I drive home and talk. It's such a relief to be away from Claire's problems for a few minutes.We talk about school and other things and for a minute, it's like our lives were normal again, like it was before last Friday.

January 23, 2004 - Claire

I hate doctor's appointments. For the past week, I have had 7. Three MRI's. The only reason I hate doctor's appointments is because of all the people around you. You all are waiting for the same thing.

To be told what's wrong with you. You just sit there, not knowing how bad it is. Doctor's appointments are never good. If you think about it, they never go "Yeah! I have bronchitis!" Anyway, in the past week my life has changed immensely. I found out I have a brain tumor (in doctor's terms) brainstem glioma. Surgery is not an option because it's too risky. I start radiation on Monday. The doctor said that this type of cancer is known to come back. But I heard of some cases where it has been two years after radiation, cancer free. I have never had so much of a health threat. The doctor's pointed out that I might not be around for my 18th birthday. But I don't believe that's the case. I will graduate from high school cancer free and I will become a doctor who will find a cure for brainstem glioma. I need God to do it. He will let me live. Everyday I thank God for letting me live to see it and pray for yet another. With my situation you need to be thankful for every thing. Actually, every person should be thankful for what they have. Because you seriously don't know how good you have it, until it is threatened. The doctors said that I don't have the normal symptoms (Yeah!). They think that the tumor may have been here for while. This is good because then it might be slow growing (which would be good). I'm just kind of nervous about it.

Waiting Room
Tick tock, Tick tock
We all sit in the waiting room, waiting
The clock ticks slower in the waiting room
5 minutes can take an hour to pass
We wait for news people only get in nightmares
Tick tock, tick tock
All of us are in the waiting room

By Claire Nelson

Friday, January 23, 2004 - Margy

Claire is in having another MRI. I'm sick of reading, so I guess I'll write.

It's funny; I was worrying about her having another MRI, all that radiation to her brain, when it hit me…DUH! Why be afraid of radiation causing cancer when she already has it? I guess it's just another sign that I'm losing my mind.

I still don't like Dr. Claire, even though she's supposed to be the top in her field. She seems condescending. And the thing that really makes me mad is that she has given me this book called "Caring For Your Dying Child," or some such nonsense. She gives it to me when Claire isn't in the room. I hide it in my backpack. When I get home, I throw it in the back of a drawer in the dining room. I never want to need this book, and I never want Claire to see it. If Dr. Claire is giving me this book at the beginning of Claire's treatment, does that mean she has NO HOPE for Claire? How can she treat someone who she believes is going to die anyway? How can she give Claire HOPE, if she has none? And Claire needs HOPE. It's what keeps her going. Speaking of hope, Ginger Bridget has really stepped up to the plate (whoever thought I'd say that about Ginger?) Besides continuing to sleep with her body wrapped around Claire's head, she follows Claire around and stays with her most of the time. The other night when I couldn't sleep, I took Ginger from Claire's head and put her under my arm. She lasted there about five minutes before she went back to Claire. I guess I've lost my dog, but it couldn't be for a better reason.

January 26, 2004 - Claire

Today radiation starts. I'm kinda nervous about it. It freaks me out that there will be lasers pointing at my head. I just don't want it to be screwed up. I want to be well! That would be awesome. And one day I will have a family of my own. I'm going to live!

January 26, 2004 - Margy

Claire starts oral chemo this week. We all got together with Dave this weekend (all 5 of us in the same room---WOW!) and talked about the pros and cons of oral vs. IV chemo. Claire wants oral so she doesn't lose her hair. I think if we make her lose her hair, she will give up. She's so strong and fighting so hard. To give her another blow will be too much. Dave agrees, too, but in his case it's probably because he doesn't think there is much hope either way.

Dr. Claire tells Claire she will have nausea as a side effect of chemo, but she'll give her medications for that. I say "Oh, sort of like morning sickness, like you get when you're pregnant?" Dr. Claire laughs and agrees. I think I like her a little better.

Friday, January 30, 2004 - Claire

I am never becoming pregnant. Everything smells so much, I can't bear it. I want to eat, but the smell gets to me. I haven't been to school all week.

My daily plan is as follows:
5:30am wake up
6-6:30am drive to Piedmont
6:30am take meds/obtain radiation
7:05am drive home with Dad or Mom.

Get home. Set alarm, sleep. Turn off alarm. Take meds. Let out dogs. Turn on alarm. Sleep. Turn off alarm, let out dogs. This is awful. I feel like a cripple. And I'm still tired at night, no matter how much I sleep during the day. No one knows the pain, this is torturing me. Because I can't describe this to them. They just don't understand how nauseousness can overcome your desire to eat. It depressed me to think I have 5 more weeks of therapy, but also relieves me because this is as bad as it gets. My body is trying to get used to putting poison in it every day. Already, I have taken 10 pills. I feel like a drug addict. People are being extremely supportive. It makes me smile anytime someone says something or does something in honor of me. It makes me feel important in this world and that people care. I feel bad for Kevin because I'm like soooo out of it. I dunno how he could like me. I mean, I'm hammered 24/7, I'm nothing to look at and I can't think of conversation on the phone. I know God will bring me though this. He always does. But, man, why do the things you want so much, have to be so hard to get. Maybe because when you earn them, it means so much more that if there wasn't a struggle at all. I wish this was easy. You know I do. I wish I could ask for a sign to *poof* me back to health, as if no sign of a tumor. But I can't. God made it so you trust in him. He let us live at the price of love. I'm going to respect that. Like they say "What doesn't kill you makes you stronger." Well, I better be the strongest 15 year old you meet. I know I'm going to get through this. With it being an "A" type tumor and they think it's been there awhile, is my hope. I'm relying on this little candle to bring me through the dark tunnel. I will shield it from the wind and keep it safe. I believe this is my miracle and I'm going to keep it, live with it, and embrace it.

February 03, 2004 - Claire

Tuesday (well, now Wednesday) 12:05. I can't sleep. It's from the steroids. I'm sick of being hungry all the time. I won't be normal. I'm reading this thing in front of me that says "Steroids cause insomnia." How ironic. I haven't even started my make-up work. But I will tomorrow. I just don't feel like I could give it my 100% best job right now. But maybe tomorrow. I'm ready for this treatment to be over. No one knows what this is like. I just want to be like everyone else. Healthy. No one knows how hard this is psychologically on me. I look like crap and feel like crap. And now I finally can say "Yeah, I feel crappy" and people understand. I no longer need to hold this illusion that I'm well. Because let's face it, I'm not! This actually takes pressure off me. I really don't want to lose my hair. Seriously. I don't want to. I think I'm going to start home schooling. Yeah! I like this because it takes pressure off me to get better and it makes it easier to cope throughout the day. I really feel this is best for me now. I honestly never thought I would have to go through this. I thought, "Well, I'm not going get cancer, it's an old people disease." You can't classify diseases as "old." I want my face back. The steroids cause me to gain weight in my face. I might be under 120 lbs, but I have a double chin (this will suck) and I will lose my hair. It gets worse by the minute. God, you must have a kick-ass plan in mind for me to have to go through this crap. I'm waiting to see what it is. If this is Hell, I'm bathing in it.

February 24, 2004 - Margy

Claire's fifteenth birthday. I hope she has 150 more. And, if she can beat this tumor, she is in for one heck of an interesting life, boy wise.

My parents are here for her birthday. We get in our usual disagreement about how Grant is as ADHD and autistic as I think he is. According to them, Grant is just brilliant, but misunderstood., and doesn't need medications. (If he's such a brilliant child, why is he in a school for the learning disabled?) It's just a never ending argument.

Dad did say something that touched me. I was saying something about how I wish I had taken Claire to the doctors sooner, that maybe they could have done something more. Dad says, in his blunt way, "Awww, Margie, don't even go there. Claire has always had headaches. No one would have done anything different." That makes me feel better.

We go to Longhorn's for dinner and come home for cake. We walk in the house and Kelsey and Fran arrive with presents and balloons. Claire lights up when they arrive. She loves gifts and people. A few minutes later the doorbell rings again and it's sweet Wesley and his mom, Candy, (Pastor Dee's wife and son) . I think Wesley has a crush of Claire. They have known each other since they were three years old. Maybe they'll date---my daughter dating a pastor's son. Talk about a direct line to Heaven---we could definitely use that.

Wesley and Candy bring a cake and some homemade "Candybread." We are all talking in the front hall. Mom, me, Claire, Hayley, Kelsey and Fran (who I can tell is impressed that we know the pastor's wife and son well enough to have them over to our house). The doorbell rings again. It's Creepy Kevin, the troubled teen who has a crush on Claire. He brings her a big, ugly, black stuffed dog.

I'm watching Kevin and Wesley to see how long it will take for them to figure out that they are each other's competition. Claire starts introducing everyone in the room and when she starts to introduce Wesley to Kevin, you can see the light go on in both of their eyes. There is an awkward silence when Claire gets done with the intros, so I say "Would anyone like cake?" chuckling to myself about these two guys.

Leave it to Claire to have a brain tumor and two guys liking her at the same time. One of them so angelic, and the other one so demonic, he's scary. What a life!

March 8, 2004 - Margy

Claire has her last radiation today. Thank God. This has been the most stressful experience, trying to get her there every day on time, trying to take care of her, trying to work to pay the bills. Susan (who had breast cancer three years ago) told me to make sure I don't forget to pay the bills. She said when she had cancer, she forgot that once. I can see how you can. There is so much to do.

Luckily, Dave has helped out with driving. After years of not being there, or helpful, he is doing whatever we need. The days I work, I drive her and he takes her home. The days I'm off, I drive her in and take her home. One day, I was off, and so tired, and Dave VOLUNTEERED to do it. I was so grateful.

Claire feels worse. I had thought she would be looking forward to the end of radiation, and that would make her feel better; but she isn't. Most days she doesn't even go to school. Susan said I shouldn't have thought she would feel better; you always feel worse at the end of chemo because your body is wearing out. Stupid me.

It's just so hard to see her sick and fighting at the same time. Dave (in his moment of exploring the "quality of life" shit) asks Claire what she wants to do most in the whole world. She thinks about it and says to me when she gets home, "I want to go Paris with you. I have always wanted to see the Eiffel Tower." She loves the French so much. So, I guess, in this case, Dave's idea was good. And, we're going to go to Paris! Somehow. I don't know how I'll ever afford to go to Paris. I can't even afford to pay my mortgage.

March 17, 2004 St. Patrick's Day - Margy

I remember when the kids were younger, and they believed in the leprechaun.

One time, Dave accidentally broke our cheap desk drawer and left it lying on the floor the night before St. Paddy's Day. When my children got up the next morning they all thought the leprechaun had done it. They were so excited that he was such a mischief maker. Holidays used to be so much fun with all three of them.

Claire is feeling a little better. She's eating more, her blood cell counts have stayed up, and some days she can make it through a whole day of school. Maybe the radiation is working. Please God, let it work. Please give us a miracle.

Claire has decided to go to Northview next year, instead of hard shipping at Chattahoochee. I want her to stay at Chattahoochee, but she's adamant about going to Northview. I have to let her make this decision, she has so few decisions she can make. It's just that if she is at CHS, she can walk to school on the days I work. It's weird to be planning next year. Do we have a next year? I pray so with everything in me. I guess we have to plan. What is the alternative? Give up?

She wants to do cheerleading at Northview, so I'm getting her extra lessons at the cheerleading place, to help her regain her balance. Actually, she can walk toe to heel again and seems pretty good. To look at her, you would never know she was sick.

Claire's friend, Lisa, is in the hospital. Claire is so worried about her. She got her a basket and took it over to her house when she got home. Claire is such a good friend, and she loves Lisa so much.

March 18, 2004 - Margy

Well, if this story doesn't beat all. My friend, Patsy, calls me and says her neighbor, Mona (I used to teach Mona's daughter doll making) has heard about Claire's condition (from Patsy, no doubt) and Mona wants to help us go to Paris. So Mona decides to "help us" by writing an email about Claire's dream of going to Paris and sending it to all the families in their subdivision. It asks the families to donate money or frequent flyer miles so Claire can go to Paris. I am very touched when Patsy tells me this story, although I feel a little embarrassed that so many people have to hear about what we are going through.

Of course, nothing is as it seems, or at least on this journey we are on. Later tonight, Shelley and Sandy call me and express their concern about this email. I say "Well, I'm sure they mean well...blah blah blah..." Finally, Shelley says "Do you want me to read this email to you?" I say "Alright."

Oh my God!

The email is titled "Claire's Last Wish." It talks about how Claire is DYING of a brain tumor and she desperately wants to go to Paris as her LAST WISH. Oh my God! It then goes on to say that Dave is a DEADBEAT ex-husband and Grant is an autistic disabled child. I am Horrified. To think that Claire might read it! Or Dave or Grant! How cruel. I'm so upset. I talk it over with Grant, Hayley, Shelley and Sandy. It's one of the few times that I'm glad that Claire is so sick that she's missing the drama swirling all around her (she's upstairs sleeping a LOT). We decide that I will call the head of the homeowner's association and tell her I want a retraction printed. I want her to say that while the letter was meant with the best intentions, there are multiple errors in it and the family wishes no more donations or attention drawn to this matter. I talk to the woman, who printed the newsletter for twenty minutes, to convince her to retract the email. I just hope neither Claire nor Dave ever finds out about this. When I talked to Dave last night, I said, "You know there is an email floating around and I hope you never see it. It was sent by some well wishers who don't have their facts straight, so if you see it, please ignore it." He says "Uh, okay." It's one of those times when I'm glad Dave is one of the quiet types who doesn't ask a lot of questions.

March 24, 2004 - Margy

It just keeps getting better and better. Today, we spend most of day at Dr. Claire's, which should have been enough punishment. No. We get home and Claire goes to bed because she's exhausted. It's about 3:30, and Wanda, a good Samaritan from our church, comes over and brings homemade cards and wildflowers from the little kids at Sunday school. Wanda and I are standing out in the yard talking about what a beautiful day it is when, suddenly, Grant hops into the green Buick, starts backing it down the driveway and hits Wanda's van on the left side. Wanda and I are yelling "Stop!" but of course, Grant doesn't hear us; he's too busy making sure he doesn't drive on the grass on the right side of the driveway. So, now Wanda's old van (well, maybe four or five5 years) has a big dent that I have to pay for.

March 27, 2004 - Margy

Claire just bought her own laptop today. Who would have thought a child of mine would ever get a laptop? I've always felt so lucky to just be able to clothe them. So many people have sent her money and gift cards. She added them up and now has $750.00, almost enough to buy a computer. Dave says he'll pay for the rest, as sort of a late birthday gift. And Dave is supposed to take Claire to get the computer this weekend. But then, he has to leave town for some meeting or other. Claire is heartbroken that she can't get her computer (she is a drama queen) so of course, I end up taking her and paying the $200.00 more that I'll never see from Dave. It's only money, I keep telling myself. I hope the people who run debt relief will believe this.

Claire is so excited. Maybe this will give her the oomph to beat this thing.

In January, she wrote a poem called "My Little Friend". It was about her brain tumor and it's really good. So, she has started writing other poems and she wants to use her computer to write them. I think she also wants to use her computer to IM her friends, but that's ok, too. Her world has gotten so much smaller than it was before she got sick. The phone used to ring off the hook, and now we can go a whole day without anyone calling. Or if the phone does ring, it's my Mom. Maybe if Claire can IM her friends, it will keep her in better touch, and make her feel better.

We have our meeting for cheerleading on the 30th. I hope she can become a cheerleader again. This means so much to her. Against

Claire's wishes, I emailed the head of the cheerleaders and told her Claire's condition.

March 30, 2004 - Margy

We had the cheerleading meeting tonight at Northview. I hope Claire makes this team. She is counting on it so much. She looks so happy when they show the girls the uniforms.

Meanwhile, on the dented van front, it is going to cost $1700.00 to get it fixed. I think Grant wishes he were someone else's son this week, I have been yelling at him so much. Grant will pay $750.00 of it out of his savings,(which actually is all his savings) but I don't know where I will get the rest. Can't work overtime anymore because Claire needs me so. She's so frightened by each new or different symptom. She just does better when I'm around. Oh well, I guess the money thing will work itself out. I have bigger worries than that.

April 8, 2004 - Claire

<u>Double Image</u>
Sometimes people will act like they feel something
Just so other people will be pleased
I used to do that
Although every time you act that way
You kinda lose a sense of self
And if you aren't careful people will notice your double image
And then ask why you act so different around them
You could cover it up with a lie
But then u will have to cover for that lie
And it turns into a network of lies
Finding yourself in there
Is like finding hay in the needle stack
EACH one hurts a little more
After a while you don't know who is who
How can you split up two people that know everything about each other
And live so peacefully
Who will society like
The real you
Or
The fake you

By Claire Nelson

April 9, 2004 - Margy

Phyllis, Dave's sister, has been here the last several days. It has been so nice, I have known her since Grant was a baby

She is the one who told me that Dave and I were going to get divorced; all those years ago, before I even knew it. I will never forget it; she had been here several days, watching us. Dave, as per usual, was mad at me, at the kids. And I was sick with a cold. We were already in marriage counseling. Finally, the last night she was here, she and I were sitting in the den and Phyllis said "You know, Dave is verbally abusing you and the children. I would like to tell him that, if it is okay with you. If he doesn't stop, he will lose you and the children." Of course, she did tell him, and it just made matters worse, and we ended up divorced 2 years later. Sometimes I wonder if it would be easier to go through this with Claire if we were still married. At least I would have another adult to lean on, and to help me make decisions.

And now, Phyllis is here, watching Claire. Does she think that Claire is dying? Does she know the future again? Does she think that this is the last time she will ever see her niece? I don't want to know the answer to that question.

April 10, 2004 - Claire

<u>Goodbye</u>
When people leave I hate it
You never know when you will see them again
Or if anything will change next time
You miss them as if they were a part of you
You wish you could go with them
You have a hard time picking up life where it was
Because you don't like life the way it is
Letting go of someone you love seems so hard
Because you never want to say "goodbye"
Why can't we all live together
Then we would never have to say "goodbye"
I guess if you never say "goodbye"
Then how can you say "hello" again
Saying "hello" again is always the best part
Because you have days to spend with this person
So when you say "good bye" to someone you love
Just think about how much fun it will be to say "hello" to them

That makes saying "goodbye" a little easier
By Claire Nelson

April 13, 2004 - Claire

"Friends"
Ever since people find out you have a problem
They are your best friend
Its amazing the assortment of "friends"
I have
I wouldn't think anything of it
Except I know they all are just pitying me
Thinking "I'm glad I'm not her "
Sometimes it hurts to think they all feel bad for me
I'm never going to be normal to them
I feel I'm lucky
No one knows how amazing it feels to me
Just to make it to school
Maybe one day I can prove to them
I'm able to do the things that they can
by Claire Nelson

April 13, 2004 - Margy

I've noticed that Claire no longer writes in her diary. She has written in her diary since she was six years old. I asked her about it and she said she has her computer, and she hasn't had time to write. Also, she is writing poems, and she likes to instant message her friends. Still, it's odd not to see her writing in her diary.

I'm at the hospital, waiting for Claire to finish getting her MRI. This is the only chance I have to write. Everything else is so crazy. This is her first MRI since she was diagnosed. Please God, let the results show that the tumor has disappeared, or at least, shrunk. Dr. Schoenfeld told us about this little boy with cancer, who went to California for surgery, and when he got there, the MRI showed the cancer was gone. If only that can happen to Claire.

We have a big week coming up. My sister, Cindy, and her husband, Paul are coming to visit and Hayley has her prom. We bought the cutest dress for Hayley and she's getting her hair done. This should be such a happy time in our life, but instead, I'm terrified all the time. Terrified that the tumor will come back, terrified that Claire will get worse, terrified that I don't have the strength to take care of her, and terrified that she will die. I don't think I have the strength or courage to go through this.

I keep trying to focus on the now, the positives. It's so hard, though, I feel like I'm living a double life. At work I'm the old me and sometimes, when I'm really busy, I forget that Claire has a life-threatening illness. But then, I leave work, and cry all the way home.

By the time I get to our neighborhood, I am done crying and paste a smile on my face and act like it is okay and things are going to be FINE. I don't know what else to do. If I acted like I feel, I would crawl into my bed, put a blanket over my head and not come out until this whole thing is over.

Claire is doing well at her tumbling, her skills are coming back. I'm also trying to deal with Grant being tested at Georgia State and getting those results so he can get special help at Gwinnett Tech. And, of course, our "weekly" visits with Dr. Claire fill up the whole day. They are helpful though. She examines Claire thoroughly and explains why she feels this way or that. It just takes so long to get to see her.

Anyway, we'll have fun with Cindy and Paul and watching Hayley go to the Prom. My daughter going to the prom! Hard to believe. And Hayley, Claire and I are going to New York in June with Paul and Cindy. Something to look forward to!

Oh, they just said Claire will be out in a few minutes. Please God, make her tumor disappear.

** Update on MRI: Basically no change, but no growth either, so I guess that's good.

April 24, 2004 - Claire

You
I love it
When you smile at me
From across the room
I love it
When I look
In your eyes
I can just tell
You love me
I love it
When you hold me tight

Like you're never going
To let go
It's nice to know
Someone that feels
The same
Where did you go?
Did you leave me?
I thought you loved me
I'm all alone
Or was there never
anyone here?

By,
Claire Nelson

April 29, 2004 - Claire

<u>World Peace</u>
What would we do if we had world peace?
People always say that's their dream,
What if it happened?
There would be no wars
No quarrels
No prisoners of war
How would we live?
Fighting is all we have known,
For centuries
But centuries of Peace
What eternal bliss
What could we possibly
Need to change about our world, now?
I know we will think of something
Because we are never satisfied
The one moment when we realized we had world peace
How would we feel
Or act
Or even speak?

By Claire Nelson

<u>Life</u>
If life can change in just an instant,
Could it instantly change back?
If you wanted someone to like you enough,

That you changed for them,
Would they really like you for you?
If you could be someone else
Would you?
Are we able to do the things we claim to do?
Do we really think what we say we think?
Do we live life the way we want to,
Or do we just pretend to be what we want to be?
Will we ever be able to admit our faults,
Or just show the illusion that we are perfect?
So many questions
Few people admit the true answers to
Only someone who truly knows their own heart

by Claire Nelson

April 30, 2004 - Claire

My Heart

It has a mind of its own
You can not control it
As much as you want to
It's your heart
Sometimes it works with your head
Other times they fight

by Claire Nelson

Boys

You primp
You freshen-up
You look your greatest
He doesn't even notice
He doesn't know what it took to look this beautiful
He doesn't understand that you don't naturally look like this
You spend your time trying to relate to him
You change yourself in ways you never knew
You are almost as if someone you don't know
He cares to the littlest amount
He doesn't realize you have changed
Everything just for him
He doesn't even want you after the changes
You cry your eyes out
You wish you could be what he wants
You don't know what was wrong with you

He doesn't realize how much he hurt you
He probably doesn't look twice
He just moves to the next girl who looks nice

by Claire Nelson

May 4, 2004 - Margy

Claire made basketball cheerleading! I'm so happy. I mean I wish it was football, but Claire said she goofed up in tryouts and almost broke her neck, so I guess basketball is fine. She's so excited. She can't wait for school to start, to get the uniform, etc. She was the old Claire for a few minutes. It was so wonderful to see her again. God, I miss her. It's so sad to see the new Claire, always struggling, fighting, to get above feeling bad.

I asked Dr. Claire if kids with Claire's tumor usually feel so rotten after radiation is finished. She said, "Not at all." Now what does that mean? According to the medical literature, after radiation they get better for a while, but then the tumor comes back with a vengeance. When does Claire get to feel better?

One of the hardest things in walking this walk is the aloneness. I wish I knew other mothers who are going through this, to talk to. I don't know where or how to meet them. At the beginning, they told Claire and I about Camp Sunshine, for kids with cancer. But Claire had seen those kids, one time when we took Hayley down to debate at Emory University, and Claire said "No! I don't want to be part of a cancer group!" (they were sort of pitiful looking) Still, sometimes I wonder if maybe we should reconsider. This is a pretty sad, lonely journey we are on.

May 7, 2004 - Claire

<u>Hope</u>
It's what gets us through
Hard times
It's what brings us from
Depression to faith
No one knows how hope
Came about
But it definitely is not

Going out of style
If you don't have hope
You don't have dreams
Every dream starts with
A little bit of hope & luck
It's always there when times get tough
It's always there when times get rough
Hope is what has brought
Me through this experience

by Claire Nelson

<u>What makes me happy</u>
Looking up at the stars at night
Seeing the glow in someone's eyes
As they get ready to go to prom
Knowing someone that you like
Likes you back
That smile you make when you know you have done something right
The way it feels to make someone happy
The look in someone's eyes when they kiss you for the first time
The feeling in your heart when you realize you know why you are on earth
Your charisma when you are getting married
Life in general
These are just the few of the many things
That makes me happy
Happiness is very plentiful
And should be this way for everything
Don't think of what you didn't get
Think of what you have instead
But seeing someone you love
Is the happiest feeling of all

by Claire Nelson

May 7, 2004 - Margy

We went to Hayley's debate banquet tonight. I sat with Shelley and Todd's mom, and for while, it's like things were normal. Like they were before Claire got sick. Claire didn't want to go and see everyone, so she stayed with Kelsey. Hayley has such a good time, bringing her friends up to see me. We all felt so happy! I don't think I realized how sad we've all become until I saw Hayley enjoying herself so much. When did life get so hard?

Claire starts chemo again tonight. It always makes her so sick and dizzy. Another long week. God, I hate chemo, but if it works, I love chemo.

We had the best time in NYC with Paul and Cindy. We stayed at a hotel on Times Square and it was fabulous. We all went shopping, to the top of the Empire State building, out to dinner, and shows at Radio City Music Hall, Rockefeller Center. All the fun stuff. Claire got tired, but otherwise was so excited. The first afternoon, she was too tired to go out, so Hayley, Cindy and I went and had a great time, and it was so nice to see Hayley so excited. What a great trip!

May 27, 2004 - Margy

I am supposed to work this Memorial Day, but Kathy told me she would work my shift since Dr. Claire has said that it would probably be Claire's last Memorial Day. Norma, a friend from our old neighborhood and her daughter, Rachel are coming from Savannah.

Claire had said "Mom, instead of waiting for people to invite us to their house for the holiday, why don't we just throw our own party?" I didn't know if we had enough friends to invite, but when we made up our list, we came up with about 25 people. It should be a fun holiday. Please God, just don't let it be my last one with my baby.

June 9, 2004 - Margy

Claire said an interesting thing the other day. She said "You know, when I first found out I had a brain tumor, I said why me?" I nodded. She went on, "But now I think, why not me?" Wise child. She has started to have more headaches, and when she is on chemo, her balance is worse. Dr. Claire thinks we need another MRI. Which is where I am now, at the hospital, waiting for Claire. God, I hate hospitals. And to think I work in one.

** Update: The MRI showed no change from previous ones. Whew! Maybe it's just the chemo screwing with her brain.

June 24, 2004 - Margy

I didn't know things could get much worse but of course, they have. My Dad went out and mowed the lawn last Friday in 94 degree heat and had a heart attack (which no one knew). He wouldn't let my mother take him to the hospital until Monday, when he couldn't breathe. Now he has pulmonary edema, too. Chuck and Cindy are there. Chuck is giving me a hard time about not coming. But Claire is due home in two days from the Dominican Republic, where she is vacationing with Dave and Hayley. I have to be here for her. She's always so excited to see me. She calls me twice a day to tell me what she has been doing and that she can't wait to get home.

I feel horrible about my Dad. The doctor's have told us he won't recover. I can't imagine life without him. He is my dad; he has been here longer than me. How can I exist if he isn't here?

June 25, 2004

Dad passed away today. I talked him a few hours before he died. I said "I love you, Dad." He said, "Take care now." This is the phrase he always says to me at the end of our phone conversations. But this is last time I will hear it from him. I can't believe he's gone. I worked today and could hardly concentrate. Claire and Hayley get home tomorrow. It will be so comforting to have them back.

June 28, 2004 - Margy

Hayley left for debate camp. It's a tough decision whether to let her go to camp or go to grandfather's funeral. Hayley says whatever I decide is okay. She's so sweet. But Hayley's life is very hard right now. Her beloved sister is sick all the time, and all her mother can do is take care of Claire. I told Hayley I thought she should go to Debate Camp. Her face lit up, so I know I made the best decision for her.

We're waiting to see Dr. Claire right now. (I think that's all I do these days), and then Grant, Claire, Ginger and I will head down to Mom and Dad's. What a sad time. It makes the divorce I went through seem like a walk in the park.

Claire and Hayley on vacation, July 2004

July 1, 2004 - Margy

We are down in HOT Florida for Dad's funeral. Mom, Chuck and Cindy have done an incredible job of arranging everything. For the service, they have chosen a beautiful urn for Dad's ashes, and a really nice photo taken when he was younger. It's the way I will always remember Dad. The service is at the National Park and it's short, but sweet. He would be so proud. Claire holds up well, but I keep thinking "Is she next?" Please, don't let that be.

July 9, 2004 - Margy

Dave is taking Claire on a mission trip with his church. I have really strong feelings about taking a sick child on a mission trip. So I call him. "Dave, I don't think you should take a child with a brain tumor to the middle of nowhere."

Dave "The middle of nowhere is ten miles away from the University of Louisiana Hospital."

Me: "Oh." Guess I lost that one.

Anyway, Claire wants to go, and what's the worst that could happen? She could die? She may anyway. The hardest thing for me is to let her go. I worry about her so much. Hayley is still at camp, so it will be just me and Grant. I hope that isn't a foreshadowing of my future.

Claire is doing pretty well, except when she's on the chemo. She got really tired in New York City, and that was hard on her because she's used to being so active. Or was. Sometimes her balance seems a bit off, but still, to look at her, you would never know. Her hair is still beautiful, her eyes are pretty and she has such a lovely smile.

July 14, 2004 - Margy

Typical Claire. She is having a miserable time on the mission trip, calling me several times a day. The sleeping bags (they are sleeping on the floor!) are uncomfortable, she's tired, she can't work very long, it's very hot, the food is terrible. She misses me. She wants to come home. She is never going on a mission trip again.

Well, tonight she calls and has done her usual Claire turnaround. She has met a boy, Ryan, and they are in love. She feels fine, she is having a wonderful time, she is enjoying helping people, she can't wait to go again, and she says she'll be sorry when the trip is over. And of all coincidences, Ryan goes to Claire's new high school, Northview, too.

This is awful to say, but it's been kind of nice to have her gone, and not to have to worry all the time. I mean, something may happen there, but I'm not there to see it. I have gotten caught up on things at home. And my worry level, since I'm not with Claire, has gone down so much. I can breathe again, if only temporarily.

July 17, 2004 - Margy

I can't believe this. Now Mom is in ICU, and the doctors are not sure she'll make it. I want to scream "What else can go wrong?" but I'm afraid I'll find out. Mom has been so brave since Dad died, trying to stay on top of things, being positive on the phone. Anyway, the doctor said she was pushing herself too hard, Dad's dying was a terrible shock to her system and she ended up having a major heart attack. This, on top of her pacemaker last year. I think Mom will recover---she's a touch old bird and they haven't run out of tricks on the medication end. I just feel so bad for her. She hates hospitals, being sick, being taken care of, just like me.

Claire came home on Saturday and had a great time on the rest of the mission trip. The whole week she was gone, she kept telling me how she couldn't wait to get home and go to our favorite Indian restaurant.

So, today we go there for lunch, get our food and sit down. Claire looks me in the eye with such love and says "Mom, I've waited all week to do this with you. I'm so happy." My eyes fill with tears. I have been so blessed to have been loved by all my children. No matter what happens, I mustn't let myself forget this.

July 21, 2004 - Margy

Back in Dr. Claire's office (where else), at least it gives me a chance to write and think. Claire listens to her CD's or plays a game. I HATE this office. All the bright primary colors of red, yellow, blue. It's set up for little kids and some Godawful cartoon show is always blaring on the TV.(whatever happened to the Disney movies, like Little Mermaid or Aladdin?)

Actually, to be perfectly honest, besides hating this office, I HATE MY LIFE. I hate seeing my daughter suffer, I hate knowing that I'm neglecting my other children, I hate not knowing how I'm going to pay the bills, or how Claire is going to feel today. I hate never being able to get away from the worry and fear about her brain tumor. I hate feeling like I'm always waiting for the other shoe to drop.

4:00 pm

We actually had a great meeting with Dr. Claire today. Claire is so excited to tell Dr. Claire about her mission trip and Ryan, that our appointment was fun. Claire is animated and happy, and Dr. Claire jumps in with her. They had the best visit they've ever had, and I feel like Dr. Claire has seen the real Claire for the first time. I hope she sees so much more of her.

July 29, 2004 - Margy

I am presently sitting on the balcony of the world's smallest condo in Hilton Head. I'm looking at the beautiful blue ocean and watching Hayley, Amelia, Claire and Keeley dive in and out of the waves. Linda, Amelia, Keeley, me, Hayley and Claire are doing our annual trek to Hilton Head. The only thing I wish is that our condo was bigger. Linda and I get the bed near the door, with all the outdoor noise; the two older girls sleep on the sofa sleeper, and the two younger girls sleep on the floor around the sofa sleeper. I don't know where we'll put Grant when he gets here, probably on the balcony, where I'm now sitting.

But, right now, the sky is blue and the wine is good and I feel free for the first time in a long time. The first day here, Claire and Keeley go out in the water and within five minutes meet two boys. Claire is like some guy magnet. Back at the ranch, Hayley and Amelia just walk around, look beautiful and don't meet anyone. Go figure! It's been relaxing here, but also bittersweet. We have all come here for the last five years, always thinking about the next year. And will there be another trip next year? The future is such a question mark.

Even though we're here relaxing, our trip and arrival were fraught with our usual drama. As we drive out of town, Mom's girlhood friend, Alice, calls me. She can't reach Mom (who is now out of the hospital and doing amazingly well) and she's worried about her. My stomach drops. So I call Mom, luckily, she answers. She didn't hear the phone ring or something. But, at least she's ok. Then, we get to Hilton Head and that evening my neighbor, Sandy, calls. She's watching my dogs while we're gone; and she has recently had knee surgery. So, Sandy lets the dogs out of their kennels, takes them outside; and Ginger, the escape artist, runs out in the yard and won't come back in for Sandy. Here's Sandy, with her immobilized knee, in the dark, trying to catch this neurotic dog. Sandy finally calls Fran (thinking Ginger will answer to her…hah!) and Fran comes over and the two of them trap Ginger in the yard. Then they bring this nutty dog inside and lock her in her kennel. At least Ginger didn't escape from the yard.

So this morning, our second morning in paradise; I have to call long distance from Hilton Head to my veterinarians to see if Ginger can stay there for the rest of the week. Luckily, they agree to take her, only not enthusiastically (they've had her before). Tony, Sandy's husband, takes her to the vets in her kennel. He goes to hand the kennel to the veterinary tech and she says, "Why don't you take Ginger out of her kennel and hold her and then hand her over to us? It is a lot less stressful on her if you hand her over." Tony says, "Uh, no thanks, just take her in the kennel as she is." Smart guy.

July 31, 2004 - Claire

<u>Mothers</u>
*I never realized
How much you loved
Us*

Until I realized
How much we take you for granted
You have been there
Since day 1
Never have you
Stopped Loving US
We treat you with disrespect, mean feelings and unthoughtful actions
And yet
You still love Us
No more
No less
You love
All 3 of us
Just for being
Us
That's true Love

Love, Claire Nelson

July 31, 2004 - Margy

So, we get home from Hilton Head today, and guess what? The air conditioning doesn't work upstairs. In fact, it hasn't worked ALL WEEK! Grant knew about it, because he didn't come to Hilton Head until Wednesday. But did he tell me about it, so maybe I could get it fixed? NOoooo!

Grant said, "Well, Mom, you have so much to worry about, I was trying to give you a break."

Me: "A break? I have to come back from vacation in the July heat with a child with a brain tumor and we have NO AIR CONDITIONING? That is not a break, Grant."

Grant, "I'm sorry, Mom."

Luckily Shelley knows this old guy who fixes air conditioning systems. When I call him at 5:30 on Saturday night, he says he's just sitting down to dinner, but he'll be over afterwards.(Hooray!)

Wendell, the air conditioning hero, arrives and he is about 70-something with grey hair, only on the sides of his head. At the top of his head, hanging at a weird angle, is a bright, red toupee. Claire and I are watching Wendell though the kitchen window as he walks to the air-conditioning unit outside. Claire says, "Do you think Wendell knows his hairpiece is on crooked?" Me: "I don't think so, which isn't a good sign for us. People who don't know their toupee is on crooked can't always fix air-conditioners." Well, Wendell does fix the air conditioner for only $100, but I have my doubts on how long the repair may last.

I'm worried about Claire and Ryan. I so want this to work out for her. She needs a boyfriend distraction. She's being so brave. But there is something weird about Ryan. He doesn't call her nearly as much as Bryan did, and he cancels their dates a lot. I'm not getting a good feeling about him, but he is cute.

August 3, 2004 - Margy

Claire is definitely having balance issues. I picked her up at the pool the other day and she's so slow getting her towel, walking to the car. I realize it's because she's trying to walk normally. Dr. Claire insists that it isn't the tumor, based on the MRI's. That it's the steroids, the chemo, the swelling of the brain, blah blah blah. But why is her balance getting worse? What is going on? What else could it be BUT the tumor? Dave calls tonight in his usual optimistic way. He is talking about how much trouble Claire had walking on their trip to Oregon. And how her arm started trembling uncontrollably on the plane home. He's sure it's the tumor, and that it's growing. God, I hope he's wrong.

We are going to Paris and London in September. Our neighbors got together and donated frequent flyer miles and money so we can go (and apparently sent a very NICE email around the neighborhood) I honestly didn't know that there were so many kind people in this world. It will be Claire, me, Hayley, Cindy, Fran and Kelsey. We're so excited and trying to concentrate on this.

School starts next week. Claire is excited. She wants to do so much. I just hope that she can.

We had an appointment with Dr. Claire the other day and I drag Hayley along. She doesn't want to go, but she needs to see what is going on.

Claire and Dr. Claire have a good meeting. Afterwards, Hayley says two profound things. First, she says, "You know, when Claire and Dr. Claire were discussing how the color of Claire's eyes changed during radiation, I kept thinking that in another life, she and Dr. Claire would have been great friends."

Then Hayley says, "I had no idea that every system in Claire's body doesn't work right." Put that way, neither did I. But Dr. Claire asks Claire about her urine (it's hard to urinate) her vision (she is seeing double sometimes) her headaches (they come and go) her bowels (she is constipated), her sleeping (she can't go to sleep without a sleeping pill), her feet (the left one is weaker than the right) she can't walk right, her hands, (she feels like she can't write like she used to). I realize that Hayley is right. None of Claire's systems work properly. I guess because I see Claire all the time, I don't see the decline? Or is it just issues with the tumor? Sometimes my kids are smarter than me.

August 9, 2004 - Margy

Claire's first day of school. I want to let the new school know about her brain tumor, but she is adamant that I not tell them. So, on the first day of school, Claire gets off the bus and they pull her aside and ask her if she is doing drugs. Because her gait is unsteady, almost like a drunken person. In typical Claire fashion she says, "No, I'm not doing drugs, I have a brain tumor." Well, that stops them short. I admire her courage on so many levels.

I have a coordinators meeting at the end of this week and it's overnight trip. I have to go, but I hate to leave the kids alone, even for one night.

August 13, 2004 - Margy

So, I'm, at my coordinators meeting and feeling guilty for being away from the children, who have told me they will be okay, and so, I go. (Claire is now 15, Hayley is 17 and Grant is 19 years old.) Our meeting is at Lake Lanier Islands and part of the meeting is that we learn how to drive a boat together. You know, like coordinators learning how to work together. Well, it's today, Friday and we're all out on this stupid boat in the middle of Lake Lanier, burning up because it's so hot. My cell phone rings and it's Beth, the nurse at the clinic at Northview. She tells me that Claire isn't feeling very well and needs to go home. I tell her where I am and I'll try to arrange for someone to pick her up. Beth asks me how I can leave my child to go to a meeting out of town when my daughter has a brain tumor and is sick. I retort, "I have never left my children before. I am always home. This is to keep my job, which I desperately need to pay the bills." I think people who have never gone through this have no idea what it is like. I call Mr. Tony (Kelsey's Dad) and he says he will be GLAD to pick Claire up. Thank God for small miracles.

August 25, 2004

Well, the green buick car is no more. Hayley was driving it the other day, to pick up a prescription for Grant; because I had take Claire to see Dr. Claire. As we finish up at Dr. Claire's office, Hayley calls and says, "Did you mean right or left on Executive Dr? " I said, "Right." She says my writing isn't clear, and she's mad at me for making her do this; I can tell by her voice. We hang up. A minute later, she calls back and I say, "Are you still lost?" She is crying. "Mommy, I got in an accident. Can you come?" So Claire and I head to North Druid Hills, instead of home.

We get there to find Hayley still crying, and her car looks totaled. The tow truck arrives and this enormous guy with large tattooed biceps crawls out of the truck. When I tell him I want him to tow the car to my house, he spits out tobacco juice and asks me what I just said. I have to tell him two more times, during which he can't understand me and I can't understand him. It turns out he just moved here from Alabama, doesn't know the area and needs one of the girls to ride with him so they can direct him to our house. I am speechless. Do I send Hayley who is still shook up and crying, or Claire who is fifteen years old and has a brain tumor? This guy, who I have not so fondly nicknamed "Popeye" stares at me while I try to make up mind. I don't know what the lesser of two evils is. Finally, Claire says, "I'll go with him". She is looking at her sister, who is crying. Will Claire be okay? Will I ever see her again? Will the police understand my predicament when I file a missing persons report for Claire?

Anyway, Hayley and I drive home. Thank God for cell phones, which I call her on several times, to make sure she hasn't been abducted by this pervert. About forty five minutes after we get home, Claire and Popeye arrive towing the car.

Later this evening, we are talking and Claire says, "Mom, it was kind of exciting riding in that great big tow truck. And it was fun, because I got to think of something other than me for a change." Always a silver lining, I guess.

August 29, 2004 - Margy

It turns out that the car is totaled, so I have it towed to a junk yard. I announce to Grant and Hayley that I can am not buying them any more cars. Grant has totaled two cars, had two minor accidents and Hayley has totaled one 1 car. I have run out of money for cars. So Grant thinks about it and says, "Well Mom, I have $600 saved; if I can find a car or truck for that amount, can I buy it?" I think of the Prism that was $3000.00 and a good car. So we are talking about little less than a third of that. A car like that can't be all bad, right? So I tell him okay.

Chemo starts again tonight. I hate these weeks. Claire always gets so much worse. When will it end? It is Hayley's senior year and I can't even enjoy it She'll graduate in May. We should be thinking about senior pictures, senior rings, senior trips. Instead I am thinking: chemo drugs, MRI's, balance issues, death. Will this ever end?

Claire got her 10th grade pictures taken last week. I hope they turn out okay. She still looks normal, but her balance isn't very good.

We had our weekly appointment with Dr. Claire the other day. Claire asks if she can come off chemo sooner than a year and a half. Dr. Claire says no. Claire says, "I hate you." Dr. Claire (not missing a beat) says "I hate your tumor." Go Dr. Claire! I am pretty impressed.

September 1, 2004 - Margy

Grant found a truck for $700.00 on the internet. He and Kaj (our neighbor who has kind of taken Grant under his wing and mentors him) went to look at it, and agreed it was a good deal. So, with my blessings, Grant buys it. What a mistake! It's a 1972 Dodge truck that is primer grey with multiple dents and holes. It's so old, there's not even a title to it. The moment I see it, I think it must be a joke, like a reject from the Jeff Foxworthy show. Besides the primer grey on the outside, inside there are cigarette butts (there is no ashtray) and broken glass all over the floor (I don't want to know where this came from). When Grant shuts the driver's side door, the window falls into the door panel. The truck has no heat, no radio, barely any upholstery, no glove compartment, the odometer doesn't work and neither do the interior lights. Of course, the odometer isn't necessary, because the truck doesn't go above 30 MPH. The bumper sticker on the back says "My Son is inmate of the month at the county jail". Fitting. It looks so nice next to our neighbors BMW. If this doesn't get us thrown out of the neighborhood, nothing will.

September 13, 2004 - Margy

We get Claire's school pictures back. She looks so beautiful. Who would ever know she has a brain tumor? She looks so normal. She's so happy with her pictures.

Claire is getting her monthly MRI. I don't know how she does it. She's the strongest person I know. I hate the MRI waiting room at Scottish Rite. It's so small and that frigging TV is always on, with more of these idiotic cartoons. It is no wonder the IQ of American children has declined. The siblings of the kids in the MRI's are always crying or crawling all over the room. I get up and go to the cafeteria, but that's no better. The food is terrible and the room is dirty. I sit there, just staring out the window at the rainy, overcast day. It all seems so hopeless.

Oh, so the Claire and Ryan update. He doesn't call her much, and she can't figure out what's going on. At school, Claire sees a girl named Katie talking to Ryan. She goes up to Katie and asks her how she knows Ryan. Katie says "I'm his girlfriend." Katie asks Claire how she knows Ryan. Claire says "I'm his girlfriend, too." That was a couple of weeks ago. So the ending is great. Claire and Ryan have a big fight and break up. Ryan and Katie have a big fight and stay together (apparently they've been dating for awhile). So this week, Claire is IMing friends when Ryan comes on. They start to talk and Ryan asks her out again. Claire IM's him: "I don't date people who date other people. Unlike you." Go Claire!

Grant's truck continues to be a source of entertainment to us all. I have never seen such a piece of ...you know. When he goes out in the mornings, it takes about ten tries to get it started. Runnn.... runnn... then he'll back out of the driveway and it will immediately stall. I can hear him from my bedroom, trying to start it again, ten more times. Later on, he'll call me, "Mom, the truck stalled at 120 and Jones Bridge. Can you pick me up?" We take the truck to Robert's Automotive to have it checked out. Now, normally, Robert is this very shy, serious person. But today he calls me, laughing, and says, "This truck has been rode hard and driven." I said "OK,(not finding the humor in the situation that he is. Of course, I own this piece of you-know-what) " Can you fix it?" He says, "How much do you want to spend?" I say, "How much do we need to spend to fix it?" He laughs again and says, "You can spend endlessly on this truck." Me: "How about $500.00....will that get it to run?" Robert: "For awhile."Great.

** Update: Claire's MRI showed no change in her tumor. There is swelling, or tumor, or no one knows, but the tumor isn't growing. How can they say that when Claire is listing to the left side and weak? Am I the only person who sees this?

Claire's 10th grade picture

September 18, 2004 - Margy

Yesterday we took our overnight flight to London and WE ARE HERE! It's so exciting to be in another country. We were all exhausted after our eight hour flight, but now we have our second wind. Poor Claire. She wants to feel better, but she doesn't. So tonight she takes a nap while the rest of us go to the Sherlock Holmes Restaurant. It's so cool, even though the food is just barely okay. Unfortunately, when we got back, Claire is awake, and we all make the mistake of telling her how much fun the restaurant was. Then she is mad that we didn't take her. This is so hard, for all of us, but especially her. Maybe it will get better.

September 21, 2004 - Margy

The rest of our trip in London turns out okay. Even though Claire and I lost everyone on Sunday so it was just the two of us (and her damn wheelchair on the cobblestones) trying to find our way back to our hotel. We laughed so much. She hates the wheelchair, but it gives her the energy to see what she wants. We went to the Tower of London and all sorts of interesting places.

Today as we're on the tube, I'm sitting with Fran, Claire and Kelsey are sitting together and Hayley and Cindy are sitting together. Suddenly, Hayley starts crying. Cindy, Fran, and I look at each other. Fran gives me such a look of compassion as I switch seats with Cindy and sit next to Hayley. I ask Hayley what's wrong. She says, "Claire is so much worse. She isn't going to make it, is she?" I say, "What do you mean?" (looking behind me to see if Claire has heard, which it doesn't appear that she has) Hayley says, "In the Dominican Republic, Claire was active all day and she wasn't tired and she used to work out all the time. And now she can't even get though the day without being tired. She's worse." I don't' know what to say. I am living with Claire every day, and I don't see the decline like Hayley does, I guess. I hug her and say, "We'll be okay." And she hugs me back. But what if she right? Is Claire failing in front of all of us? Is there something else I can do?

September 22, 2004 - Margy

We are in Paris! Claire is so excited. It's such a neat city, even if the people are rude. . We went to the Louvre yesterday, which was an all day trip. But, tonight is a night I will always remember.

Claire has wanted to go to the Eiffel Tower since we got here, it is her dream to see it up close. But, every time we get ready to go, something happens. Anyway, tonight, we decide to go to the Eiffel Tower in spite of the unrelenting rain, because we are leaving tomorrow and it's our last chance to see it up close. We all catch cabs to get there, and don't take the wheelchair.

When we get there, the Eiffel Tower is lit up with a million lights. It looks like a fairy tale. Because of the rain, there aren't many people there, just all these guards with camouflage on and big machine guns. UGH!

Cindy, Hayley, Claire, Kelsey and I take the elevator to the top (Fran is afraid of heights and stays on the ground). When we get to the top, we can see all of Paris and we're on top of the EIFFEL TOWER. Suddenly, Claire has realized her dream and she starts laughing and enjoying herself, like I haven't seen her do in a long time. She is the old Claire. She laughs, and twirls herself around a pole. She's so happy, she wants her picture taken, she buys souvenirs for everyone. She wants this moment to last forever. I only wish it could.

Kelsey, Fran, Claire, Hayley and I in Paris, 2004

September 25, 2004 - Margy

We are on the plane back to the U.S. Claire and I are sitting together, Hayley is next to Claire. Claire turns to me and says, "Mommy, I can't feel my left side." My stomach drops. I just stare at her. I don't know what to do. Finally I say, "We'll call Dr. Claire when we get back, but it will be okay." Will it?

September 27, 2004 - Margy

We're back on U.S. soil. Today we have a meeting with all of Claire's teachers to help adapt her curriculum to her physical limitations. This is called an IEP (interventional education plan.) I remember when I used to do these with Grant. That was because he was learning disabled. Who would have ever thought we would have to do it with Claire? Life is cruel.

Claire is amazingly mature. She tells the teachers what she needs. That she can't make it to first period, she's too tired in the morning. That she needs times when she can rest during the day. Beth, the clinic nurse, is there. She's so nice and very supportive of Claire. She says that Claire can come to the clinic anytime she wants. Thank God for kind people. And to think I so misjudged her back on Lake Lanier. Claire's math teacher is rather cruel when he says he doesn't know what Claire needs, since he has only seen her twice. This is because she's too tired to make it to first period. I want to say, "Maybe you'll be kinder when you live longer and see the blows that life can give you." At the end, we work out a plan for Claire and she's happy. As happy as you can be, knowing that you have special needs.

October 7, 2004 - Margy

Claire's balance has been steadily going downhill. So, Dr. Claire finally suggests a physical therapist. Today we meet Dana for the first time and she and Claire instantly bond. Thank God. Claire has been so upset about doing physical therapy; maybe this will make it easier. I see all these little kids that can't balance or are retarded. I thought I had it tough with Grant, but I guess not. At least he could walk and talk (well, he couldn't talk too well, but after speech therapy, he was a lot better)

I am finding more and more that I wish I knew another mother who was going through this and could talk to me. Shelley is the best, and listens to me almost every night. But, thankfully, she can't really relate. I need someone who is living this nightmare. I am thinking about Camp Sunshine again.

October 11, 2004 - Margy

Today Claire meets with an occupational therapist, Chris. She works at the same place as Dana, so they can have appointments back to back. Whoopee!! Whoever thought I would think this is neat?

October 13, 2004 - Margy

Homecoming is this weekend. I can't believe it, but Claire, with her poor balance and brain tumor, has a date. His name is Danny and he's on the football team. Apparently they are in chemistry class together. He has never been on a date before. She's so excited. She's wearing her beautiful cranberry dress from last year.

October 15, 2004 - Margy

Today is the Homecoming game. Claire stayed home late this morning so she can make it through the game. She has her cute cheerleading outfit on. It's so sad. Claire wants to be normal more than anything in the world. Why can't she be?

Anyway, Claire calls me from school, she's so happy and having a fabulous time. Hayley and I go after school and watch the floats and film Claire on her truck with the other cheerleaders. She is smiling and waves at us.

Tonight, she calls me at about 8:30, in the middle of the Homecoming game. She needs to come home. She's too tired and needs me to come and get her. So I drive to Northview and try to park in the parking lot where she's to meet me. A cop comes up to me and says, "You can't park here. It's closed." I say, "I don't want to park, I only need to pick up my daughter who is waiting somewhere in this lot for me. She's feeling sick." He says, "I'm sorry lady, you aren't allowed in here." I take a deep breath, I am starting to panic. "Look, my daughter has a brain tumor and she's sick and she's waiting for me to pick her up in this lot." He looks at me like I have sunk to a new low to make this up. I say, "This is the truth," and my voice starts to break, "I would do anything if it weren't the truth, but she does have a brain tumor." He looks at me and waves me through the gate. I find Claire with her friends and we drive home.

October 16, 2004 - Margy

The Homecoming Dance is tonight. I take Claire to her friend Cameron's house to have her picture taken. There she is, with Kelsey, Kristen, and Cameron, the friends she's had since the second grade. And Claire is leaning to the left. She doesn't look very well.

Kristen is moving to Michigan after today. Sue, Kristen's mother, starts to talk about the move and then she looks at Claire and her voice breaks and she starts crying. Sue says "I'm so sorry; I didn't mean to get emotional about this move." She says "move" but we all know that what she means is about seeing Claire like this.

Sue has known Claire since she was seven years old. She has picked Claire up from swim meets, gymnastic events, she has had Claire over to sleepovers at her house. Claire and Kristen were in Brownies and Girl Scouts together and even went to camp one year. She has told her daughter, Kristen (who has ADHD) that she should be more like Claire. And now, she is crying for Claire.

Luckily, Claire doesn't notice this, with all the picture taking and people here. But I do. Everyone feels so bad about Claire; me most of all. If only there was something we could to make this nightmare go away.

Anyway, Claire and Danny are going to Homecoming. Since this is his first date ever. We decide that I'll pick up Danny at his house and his parents will bring him and Claire home.

Hayley, who has nothing else to do, says "Well, I'll go along with the two of you. With you and Claire, it's never dull." Little does she know.

Claire, Hayley and I drive over to Danny's house. It's in the country and we keep driving to more and more expensive neighborhoods. Finally, we reach Danny's. His house has stone lions on each side of a large circular driveway, a pool is in the back. Leave it to Claire to get the guy who lives in the several-million-dollar home. We park in the circular driveway with the Mercedes, a $50,000 brand new truck and two others cars of lesser distinction. I tell the girls his parents probably won't talk to me in my cheap, little Toyota Matrix. We go into his house and his parents are so nice. We talk about what a nice neighborhood this is. Danny's father says, "Well, it better be, my brother built it and he only builds good houses. Only our family lives on this street." There are four other lovely homes. Danny is so sweet, he bought Claire a corsage. On the way to Homecoming, I hear them talking in the backseat. Claire says "I'm so excited about this dance. I love to go to dances." Danny: "Oh, yeah, me too." Claire "I mean I wish they had dances more than once a year. You know, like a Homecoming dance in the fall and then another one in the spring." Danny: "Oh, yeah, me too." Liar, but he is sweet.

October 28, 2004 - Margy

Today, Joel, one of the nurses I work, says, "Well, Margy how was your day off?" I snapped and said, "Horrible. I had to take Claire to the oncologist, the physical therapist and the occupational therapist." Joel just looks shocked. I didn't mean to snap at him. It's just that my life isn't my own anymore. It's an endless saga of more and more doctors/ PT/OT/MRI appointments. Will it ever end?

October, 29. 2004 - Margy

Claire, Kelsey and Ali are having a sleepover. They're watching "Peter Pan." In the middle of the movie, when Tinkerbell dies, Claire starts to make loud noises. I hear her and come in the room to see what's going on. I can't tell if Claire is sobbing or laughing, I have never seen her like this. I look at Kelsey, and I can tell that she can't tell either. Finally, Claire says she's really crying, she isn't laughing. We all stand by her, and put the movie on hold while she gets control of herself. My heart breaks for her. Does she think that this is her future? Does she think she's Tinkerbell, like she used to when she was a little girl? What can I do for her? How do we cope with this?

Halloween, October 31, 2004 - Margy

Thank God it's on a Sunday this year, so I don't have to worry about taking off. Halloween has, traditionally, always been such a fun holiday. Every year it was so busy, trying to get the kids' costumes (that I make) ready in time, get the candy, go out with them, ring the doorbells, and give out the candy.

One night, when she was little, Hayley said, "Mom, wouldn't it be neat if every night was Halloween, and every morning was Christmas and every afternoon was Thanksgiving?"

Last year, I made Claire a Renaissance costume out of this dark green velvet material. She looked so pretty, and she and Kelsey went out trick or treating. This year she doesn't want to. She can't walk well enough, and is embarrassed.

We had the worst thing happen the other day. Claire and I were in Burger King, getting a coke. And we saw Bryan's mother, Tammie, drive by in her van---she was waiting at the drive through. She had been Claire's cheerleading coach in 8th grade. Claire says, "Oh, Mom, I don't want Miss Tammie to see me like this." She doesn't talk much about how she feels about how she looks, but I know it breaks her heart. We waited until we thought Tammie was gone, and then we walk out. There's Tammie, staring at us through her van window, with this look of horror on her face. At least Claire was spared that, she was too busy looking straight ahead and trying to get to the car.

November 2, 2004 - Claire

I feel like a baby. I can't do anything by myself and I hate it. Taking kindness from others when you're used to doing stuff yourself is hard. I'm so sick of not feeling my left side, being felt sorry for, constantly being cared for, reading with one eye, not being able to walk, not being able to be myself, taking steroids, not being able to do cheerleading like I want to, not being able to dance, looking fat, feeling so trashed, all the time. Always worrying, have everyone preach to me. Crying so much and there is so much more, but my sleeping pill is kicking in, so going to bed now.

November 10, 2004 - Margy

School has been in session for about three months and our life has fallen into its usual school pattern. Not the pattern any of us would have picked, but a pattern nonetheless. Grant attends Gwinnett Tech at night and likes going there. The people fascinate him, as they're older, more experienced in life. He likes his landscaping classes. Once again, he hates his job at the pizza parlor. Will he ever find a job he likes? He hated working at the nursery, mowing lawns. Seems like the only thing he likes to do is build ponds (as testified by my enormous pond in the backyard). He is socially slow, so maybe if he continues to plow ahead, he will find a career path and social contacts he likes. He has started to become friends with Rob, a nice kid at the pizza parlor. That's progress. Unfortunately, he is also friends with Andrew (also of pizza parlor fame) who is a recovered (?) heroin addict and always late for work.

Hayley is enjoying her senior year as much as anyone can in our circumstances. She's busy with debate and the typical senior stuff. She has a new boyfriend, Mark, who lives in New Hampshire (of all places, met him on a debate trip). We're supposed to meet him sometime soon. She seems happier than she's been since Claire was diagnosed, so that's good. She is on the phone all the time with Mark. It's kind of funny to see (or hear).

And Claire. Everyday is an adventure, not necessarily a good one. She tries to go to school when she is up to it. If I'm at work, Mr. Tony (Kelsey's dad) drives her. I HATE to ask others for help, but all of them, Kelsey, Fran and Tony, are always so willing to do what we need, and I'm so grateful for that. I schedule Claire's doctor /PT/OT/MRI or whatever on my days off. If it's a decision-making appointment, Dave will come. We see Dr. Claire either once or twice a week, and Dave's been with us twice since she was diagnosed. Even though Dave is a physician, he never liked patient care, which is why he went into research. He has never liked being around sick people, and now that it is own daughter, I don't think he can deal with it. Still, Dave takes

Claire to dinner each Wednesday, and has started to take her to lunch on Sundays If Hayley is in town, she joins them.

But for most of the appointments, it's just Claire and me. We spend a lot of time together, especially after Grant and Hayley have gone to school. I haven't spent that much time alone with any one person since I was first married! Yet, it's nice, even if we wish we weren't walking this walk. Claire is fun to be with, upbeat, and fun to talk to. Always looks on the bright side. For the most part, I don't feel resentful that I have given my present life to her. Like when she (and Grant and Hayley) were little and needed me so much.

Ginger continues to take care of Claire, she follows here everywhere, even into the bathroom, where she'll sit on Claire's lap if she'll let her. I've never seen a dog so devoted.

Tomorrow night I'm dragging Claire to Camp Sunshine so we can meet other children going through what we're going through. She's not thrilled about going, but her world has become so small, so narrow, she's willing to do anything. For me, I need to talk to some other adults going through what I am before I lose what's left of my mind.

November 11, 2004 - Margy

Well, the white trash truck is no more. Claire wasn't feeling well, and needed to come home from school, and Grant was off, so I sent him to pick her up. I told him to just pick her up and bring her home. What part of that he didn't understand, I don't know, He did pick her up, and then convinced her he should give her a driving lesson in that piece of you know what. Her, with her weak left side! So, they drove out to the country and she drove the truck right into a ditch. They're lucky they weren't killed. Grant had to call a tow truck and the place they towed it to said the truck was too old and broken to fix. So I thought, do something nice for someone else. Donate it to the church. Maybe some mechanic or teenager will have fun repairing it. I called the church. They don't take car/trucks built before 1980. So there it is, stuck at this repair place. I think I'm going to just leave it there. It would cost more to move, and they don't know our name (I never had time to have the handwritten title changed).

My Mom is going to buy the kids another car. She was the one that bought the green LeSabre, too. Bless her heart. Will this car issue never end?

We went to Camp Sunshine tonight. Thank God! What a wonderful experience to be with others who are walking my walk. I dropped Claire off, did a few errands, and then went into the library to wait for Claire. This woman, Patti Phillips, walks in. She had the kindest face. Her daughter, Stephanie, has been battling Ewing's Sarcoma for years. Patti just found out today that there is no more hope or treatment for Steph. She is going to have to put her in hospice. She said this calmly, bravely. I said "I'm sorry." I guess this is what cancer does. It takes people who are total strangers and gives them an instant bond-- where they can just meet and then tell each other their most private experiences and feelings.

Then, another woman, named Nancy Olson, comes in a few minutes later. She, too, has the kindest eyes. Does childhood cancer made us kinder? Or is it because we are in the same boat that we understand each other better?

Nancy's son, Will, has a medulloblastoma (brain tumor) and is presently going through stem cell transplant. The three of us chatted, and I learn that Will is also a patient of Dr. Claire's. Maybe I'll run into them there. Nancy gives me her phone number.

I left Camp Sunshine feeling so uplifted. I am not the only parent on the entire planet going through this. And Claire liked it, too. They gave her a camera to take pictures of her life and share with the group. She was most excited about the camera. Go figure. We are going to Camp Sunshine for their Thanksgiving dinner in two weeks.

November 15, 2004 - Margy

Another MRI today. When Dr. Claire calls tonight, she says it looks like there is a cyst on Claire's brainstem and we need to watch it to see if it's growing. She suggests we make an appointment to see the dreaded Dr. Hudgens to consult him about the cyst. Good news: No growth of tumor.

November 19, 2004 - Margy

We meet with Dr. Hudgens. Dave comes, too. Dr. Hudgens says there is a cyst, but presently it isn't pressing on anything important in the brain (is there anything in the brain that isn't important?) However, if the cyst continues to grow, he will have to go in and drain it. **BRAIN SURGERY!** My heart stops. She could die! He tells us the cyst might subside by itself, but mostly likely, it will need to be operated on. On the way home, Claire is her usual brave self; she's going to pray that the cyst goes away on its own; she believes it will.

I'm think I'm having a panic attack (Atlanta traffic isn't helping) I'm trembling, I can't catch my breath, I'm nauseous, my palms are sweaty. I'm a nurse, I know I'm suffering from anxiety, and I also know that I need to calm down before Claire starts to notice how distraught I am. But I can't and it's the most anxious ride home ever. Luckily, though, I don't think that she noticed. She was busy talking about the pros and cons of surgery.

This evening, though, Claire says, "Mom, have you calmed down yet, because you were a real mess in the car today. I was worried about you." So much for hiding my feelings.

Thanksgiving, November 25, 2004 - Margy

We decide to have a great big old Thanksgiving, like we do every other year when I have the kids. Claire says she wants to be home and have a "Big Turkey Day." My mom flies up from Florida and we invite Susan and Shelley over. I even invite Dave, but he has made plans to see his sister, Shay, in Florida.

We have a great dinner and so much fun. It is fun to entertain; I wish we did it more. Claire is even perkier than usual. It must be awful to always feel sick. Her balance has been getting worse and her left sided numbness comes and goes, but I guess now we have a reason: it is the cyst.

Claire likes me to massage her left leg a lot, and that seems to help the circulation. Sometimes, though, her left leg is so cold to the touch. She has been falling more, but refuses to use the cane I bought her, or the walker. I don't blame her. My mom is here and doing well. She's very pleasant and grateful to be able to spend Thanksgiving with us. I know this is so hard for her without my dad, but she brightens up around the children.

November 25, 2004 - Margy

Today I worked, and Hayley was in charge of Mom and Claire. When, I get home from work at 8:00 at night, Hayley throws my credit card at me (I had given it to her to shop) and yells "I'd rather be at school then have to go through this day again!" She stomps off. Claire is sitting in the kitchen when this happens and I give her a 'what was that all about?' look.

Later, as we are getting ready for bed, I ask Claire how the shopping went. Claire tells me how Hayley had to get her up, help her dress, go over to the hotel and get grandma and bring her back. Then she had to help Claire get into the car. So, they decided to go to the grocery store. When they got there, Hayley parked the car, helped Claire inside (in the rain) and helped Claire get in the little motorized shopping cart. Then Hayley had to walk slowly around the store with Mom. Meanwhile, Claire is in the motorized cart, (which she doesn't drive too well, due to her left sided weakness) and she accidentally ran into a display of Barbie dolls and they flew all over the place. The manager wasn't very nice about it because she thought that Claire did it on purpose (because to look at her, she doesn't look like she belongs in a wheelchair). So Hayley had to help the manager put the Barbie's where they belonged, then help Grandma and Claire back to the car. Then Claire wanted a Coke, so Hayley stopped at Burger King, She buys a coke for herself and Claire in the pouring rain. As Hayley is passing the Coke to Claire, Hayley's Coke (that she had sat on the car roof) slides off and spills on the ground. Hayley is so mad.

As Claire is seriously telling me this story, I can feel the edges of my lips start to curl up. This is one of the funniest stories I've heard all day (well, I do work in an ER after all) and both she and I start to laugh and can't stop.

November 30, 2004

We meet with Dr. Hudgens again. Claire's symptoms are worse; the Cat scan shows the cyst is growing. She needs surgery. They schedule it for December 3, 2004, the day after my birthday. At least, I can stay in the hospital with Claire the whole time. I can't imagine being without her.

Claire will be in ICU the first night. Dr. Hudgens is very nice and reassuring. She will be okay, he says. It's nice of him to say that, but it's not easing my terror.

December 2, 2004 - Margy's Birthday

For my birthday, Claire gives me this poem:

Devotion
I know you will be there
When I fall

I know you will be there
To wipe my tears away
You would do anything
For me
When we get bad news
The first thing you say is
"It's going to be ok"
You say we are in this
Together
It's tough to believe sometimes
But we really are in this
Together
You have been there
Every step of the way
And I know your not going
Anywhere
I wouldn't have made it here
Without you
You are truly
Devoted
To Mommy with love,

Claire

December 3, 2004 - Margy

I'm in the ICU waiting room, waiting for them to tell me how Claire is doing. She has been in the OR for about two hours. They are so nice here, and they call every hour to let you know how she's doing. Dave is here, too, and we're doing our usual good job of avoiding each other, but acting like we're not doing that.

I had such a nice birthday yesterday. Grant, Hayley, Claire and I went out to dinner at Longhorn's, and then when we got home, Laura came over with a gift, then Shelley, and finally, Fran. It was so sweet. Usually just the kids make a fuss of my birthday.

** 4:00pm: Claire made it through OR with flying colors. They put a shunt in to keep the fluid draining so that the cyst will continue to shrink and eventually disappear. When Claire woke up, she could feel her left side! so maybe it will work. Claire and I are in ICU, but I think a more appropriate name would be: "Intensive Sleep Deprivation Unit." I mean, I've worked in ICU's, but this is terrible. The staff is very nice, but there is the probably brain damaged child who lets out with an ear piercing scream every 45 minutes and doesn't stop until they medicate him. I heard one nurse say, "They've got to up his Ativan." Amen. Then, if the kid isn't screaming, Claire's pump is going off, or the monitor or the ventriulostomy pump. I think I've slept a total of one half hour, since 10:00pm last night.

Claire is okay, a little nauseated, weak, but answers questions and smiles. I never thought I would love to see her smile so much.

December 6, 2004 - Margy

We are home!! Thank God. What a nightmare staying in the hospital is. I guess because Claire has been on oral chemo for so long, we haven't had to be in the hospital until now. Something I will never miss. But we are home and Claire feels pretty good. She is still weak on the left side, but compensating, like she always does. I'm so glad she's feeling better.

December 11, 2004 - Claire

I'm really sick of my life. I'm embarrassed to be with myself. I look fat, am really moody, my eyes are screwed up and I'm just embarrassed to walk, talk, sit, stand, and know myself. I have headaches every day and it's annoying. My neck hurts from my surgery, and the stitches look like Frankenstein's head. At lunch when I have the wheelchair, I eat in the clinic to avoid questions and annoyance.

I am so sick of people acting like I am their special baby. Especially Mary, Mom's friend. She annoyed the Hell out of me. She does NOTHING. I do nothing or at least try to be productive, but she has had it all taken away before, so you would think she would appreciate it a little more. She smells and my room smells awful! She is constantly talking about her "gastric problems" which no one cares about. She just gets on my last nerve.

December 14, 2004 - Margy

We had Camp Sunshine last Thursday, and Claire and I went. She actually had fun and enjoyed meeting the kids that were there. I was in a parents' group and I saw Patti Phillips and Nancy Olson again. Nancy and I have run into each other at Dr. Claire's (I guess she's there as much as us, so now we look for each other. It makes the visit almost fun. There was also a man there who had lost his wife to cancer and now his daughter has a brain tumor, but is doing well.

We meet with Dr. Hudgen's today and he seems a little disappointed that Claire isn't doing better. She's still so weak on her left side, even though some feeling has come back. No one can tell me why.

He took out her scalp staples. Claire is upset because her vision is still double and Dr. Hudgen's said it may take a while for that to clear up. He did give us the name of a pediatric ophthalmologist. Oh, great, another doctor.

Still, I have to admire Claire. Since she's been sick, she has taken on more household chores, like putting away the laundry. She said, "I just feel better if I do something to help you, because you're helping me so much." I don't know if I could handle this situation with the grace and courage that she has shown.

December 15, 2004 - Margy

Claire and I are at Dr. Claire's today. They have a Christmas tree decorated with Aflac ducks. Claire keeps commenting that our dog, Ginger, loves Aflac ducks. As we wait for the elevator, we stand in front of the duck tree. Claire says again, "Ginger would love one of these Aflac ducks." The sign on the tree says: "Please do not take ducks off the tree". I say to Claire, "I'm not stealing a duck from a Christmas tree for sick children, to give to a dog."

Claire thinks about it and says "Ok, Mom." Then, a few minutes later she says "Mom, I am a sick child, and my dog would LOVE that duck!" She then takes a duck off the tree and puts it in my pocket (since my pockets are bigger than hers). We both look at each other and start to giggle like school girls. We giggle all the way home.

Ginger, the dog, is so excited to get her new duck. It is so funny about Claire and Ginger. She used to hate Ginger, but since she's been sick, Ginger has been her best friend. Ginger has been with Claire all the way, sitting with her, sleeping with her body wrapped around Claire's head. Ginger has become Claire's dog, instead of mine. I think that Ginger is her best buddy.

December 18, 2004 - Margy

Claire has been discouraged lately. After we get home from Dr. Claire's, I find Claire sitting on her bed. She says, "I can't go through this anymore. I'm not strong enough." I sit next to her. "What do you mean?" I say, like an idiot. She says, "I just don't think I have the strength to get through this anymore." Me: "Oh." I am literally at a loss for words, because I don't think I have the strength to get through this either, and I don't know what to say to encourage my beloved child. Hayley gets home from school. I call to her to come up and join us. I tell her what Claire has said and she just stares at both of us. She doesn't know what to say either. Finally, I hear the front door open and it's Grant. I tell him to come up to Claire's bedroom, and for a change, he comes the first time I call. I then tell him what Claire said, and does he have anything to say to her? I'm thinking, please Grant, save me here and I will forgive all of your endless transgressions. He thinks for a minute and says, "Well, Claire, it's a little late for giving up, isn't it? I mean if you were going to give up, you should have given up in the beginning, before it got tough, instead of now, after you have put so much into it." All of us looked at Grant, stunned. Hooray! I knew there was a decent human being in there somewhere, and he picked the best time of all to show it. Claire thinks about what he says and starts to talk; in fact, we all do and we end up feeling so much better.

Later tonight, Claire and I are sitting in the den. I ask her if she would do something for me. "Will you do this? Do you trust me?" I say. And she says "Mom, I will do anything for you." I love her with my whole heart. Then I say, "I'm just so sorry you have to go through this." She says, "I'll stay as long as I can."

December 19, 2004 - Margy

Hayley's 18th birthday. I can't believe my daughter is 18! Where did the time go? Last year, I didn't know what to do for Hayley's birthday, and Claire said that we should have a surprise party for her. So, last year, Claire and I pretended Hayley's birthday wasn't anything special and secretly invited all of her friends to a "French Crepe Birthday Luncheon Party" This was Claire's idea, and Hayley loved it.

This year, I can't think of anything to do, (my mind is blank a lot these days) but Hayley's friends, Brittany and Maggie, come up with their own idea. They take Hayley to Chuckie Cheeses and then bring her back home to decorate cookies. Maggie even brings her own cookie dough and decorations.

I take videos of Hayley in her apron, getting the dough ready, and Claire, Maggie and Brittany, sitting at the table, ready to decorate the cookies. They all look so happy, even Claire, who it is obvious; can't use her left hand. Claire is half smiling and enjoying being with her sister and her friends.

December 25, 2004 - Margy

Christmas. Was there ever one so bittersweet? Dad is off, on the sidelines, watching all of us from above. Claire is here, but for how long? Mom is doing well, but when will that end? Cindy, Paul, Chuck and Mom bought Claire, Hayley and I gift certificates to get massages, nails and all sorts of things done at the spa. Claire loves it. Then Cindy and Paul give Claire and Hayley this wonderful memory board of our trip to Europe. All three of my children look happy with their gifts. I've been through the saddest Christmas of my life (when Dave wasn't speaking to me) and the happiest Christmas of my life (when I was little or my children were little). I have had so many Christmases, but never one like this.

December 31, 2004 - Margy

To think that only a year ago, we were so normal, so boring. I wish we were boring again. Anyway, Katie, Claire's friend, comes over and spends New Year's Eve with Claire and me.

Grant is at a party and Hayley is on a Debate trip. Katie is so sweet to Claire. And you can tell that Claire eats it up. She's so lucky to have Katie, Lisa, Kelsey, and Ana-they're the best friends anyone could have.

I go over to a neighbors house for a New Year's Eve Party. It's a nice party, but I want to be home with Claire. I get home right before midnight and Claire, Katie and I welcome in 2005 in together.

What will this year bring? Do I really want to know? No. Just let it happen.

January 13, 2005 - Claire

In observance of Martin Luther King's Birthday Claire writes:

" I dream one day I will be cancer free. People won't look at me and feel bad for me. I won't need help with such simple things as tying my shoes. Every time anyone hears a crash, they don't immediately think it is me falling. My bruises will go away. I will be able to walk, tumble and cheer. I can go running on my own without a supervisor.

Each child with some kind of childhood disease fights it with all their hearts and never gives up.

One day, the cure for cancer is found."

Claire Nelson

January 14, 2005 - Margy

It was an ordinary day....isn't that the way they all begin? We had our appointment at 10:00 a.m. with Dana, Claire's physical therapist.

When I get her up, Claire is like a wet noodle. It takes me an hour to get her dressed, she's like a newborn baby. Finally, I get her downstairs (I'm still not sure how) and into the car. The whole way to Dana's I'm thinking "Should I call Dr. Claire? Am I panicking? Is this as bad as it looks?" The sad part is I don't know anymore. I'm a nurse, but I can't heal my daughter, and I can't tell if she's getting worse or better. We get to Dana's and when Dana sees Claire wobbling in, her smile turns to one of horror. I say, "Thanks, Dana, I needed that look to know whether to call Dr. Claire or not. I'll call her while Claire is in with you." I am trembling. I get Dr. Claire immediately and she says, by all means to bring Claire in. Dana and I get Claire packed in the car and we head down to Scottish Rite..

I try to reach Dave, but can't. He doesn't have a cell phone, and he doesn't answer his work or home phone. I leave him a message. I need to tell someone what is going on. I call Mr. Tony (Kelsey's dad) and he's so kind. He will tell Fran and Kelsey, he says. Finally, I call Shelley. She starts to cry. I say we'll l be okay, I just wanted someone to know. I feel so alone.

We get the MRI. The cyst is back, bigger than ever and pushing on her brain stem. Dr. Hudgen's comes in the ER. He thinks we can wait until Monday to have surgery, but he wants Claire in the hospital to observe her. Didn't we go through this last year at the same time---Martin Luther King Holiday. And once again, Hayley is on a debate trip.

Claire is admitted to Scottish Rite. I run home to get us clothes. It is 5:00p.m. traffic on Friday, in Atlanta. So, what would normally be an hour round trip, becomes a three-hour round trip. I feel so bad leaving Claire for so long and when I get back, one of the nurses is sitting with her.

Apparently, you aren't supposed to leave your child without a member of the family present. Well, who would that be? I don't know where Dave is, Hayley is out of town and Grant is at work. I don't have another member of the family.

Claire and I spend Friday and Saturday night at Scottish Rite. The nurses are so nice. It's like Claire and I are in our own little world. Please let this world go on forever. Sunday morning we get up and the doctor on call, Dr. Janus, pokes his head in, but we're still in bed (it is after all, only 6:00a.m.). So he says he'll be back. So I think (and tell Claire) that I'll take a shower quickly (thinking he will be back in like twenty or thirty minutes) Well, I walk out of the shower, in my cute little towel and there is Dr. Janus. How embarrassing! I feel like Susan in Desperate Housewives. But the good news is, he tells us that Claire can go home for the day, if she is back by 6:00p.m.

No problem there. We rush and get dressed and drive home. Meanwhile, Claire has called Lisa, Katie and Kelsey. By the time we get home at 1:00pm, they're all there, waiting for her. She is so happy. Fran is there, too, and we all sit in the den and just talk. Claire is so happy to be with her friends and dogs. Can this go on forever?

We leave home at 5:00pm, so that we'll be back by 6:00, which we are. Claire is content. Pastor Dee arrives with Wesley (his son) for a visit. There's Claire, with her pink quilt, her pink pillow; it's sort of a pink room, and so happy. We all talk and laugh. Maybe this will all work out.

January 15, 2005 - Margy

As per Nancy Olson's instructions; Claire and I decide to set up Claire's CaringBridge site. I think of how my mother will like this. How she can check our site and see how Claire is doing, and not call me twice a day. I mean, I know that she's worried, but not much changes in a day. Claire and I sit in the computer room at Scottish Rite and here is what we write:

Caring Bridge Entry:
Saturday, January 15, 2005 9:44 AM CST
Claire is 15 years old and was always a very active child. From the time she was 3, she took ballet and tap. She was so flexible and good at dance, that her school put her in a contortionist class when she was 7 years old. That was also

the same year she developed migraines and her parents got divorced. Claire continued on with dance, tumbling and swimming and was frequently first in butterfly in swimming. She also loved school and had many friends.

In the fall of her freshman year, Claire became a football cheerleader and she joined the debate team. She had an undefeated record in debate and loved being a football cheerleader. Her cheerleading team beat the JV and won first place in competition.

For Christmas, 2003, our whole family went on a cruise to the Bahamas and Claire had a great time.

However, Claire's headaches, which she had had for years, began increasing in the fall and winter of 2003. In January, 2004, we got a Cat scan and on January 16, 2004, she was diagnosed with a glioma of the brainstem. Claire wasn't given a very good prognosis, but she is a fighter. She had radiation and chemo for 6 weeks, and she continues to have oral radiation once a month. She was doing well enough last spring to compete for cheerleading and she made it on to the basketball cheerleading squad of her high school.

Summer Claire took several trips with her family and had a great time. By fall, she was developing a pronounced weakness on her left side. In November, the MRI showed that Claire had a cyst of dead tissue in her brain. In December, that was removed and she started to improve.

Claire has been having increased difficulty with walking and yesterday I brought her into the Emergency Room and a Cat scan showed that her cyst had returned. She will have to have surgery to remove the cyst on Monday, January 17, 2005. The good news is that the MRI showed that the tumor hadn't grown in a year, so that is something to be happy about. Please pray for Claire on Monday when she has her surgery.

I try to sound so upbeat for this CaringBridge site, but I keep thinking; I'm only trying to put a positive spin on a very sad time. That's all I can do.

January 17, 2005 - Margy

Claire's SECOND brain surgery. Fran comes to the hospital, and we wait together to hear how Claire is. A pastor from John's Creek, Chris comes and sits with us. We invite Dave (who is at the other end of the room and pretending we don't exist) to join us. We all have a nice prayer. If only it will work. Finally, after two hours, Claire comes out of surgery. She looks so much brighter than she did the first time. They take her into ICU Hell (my term) and the nurses say, "Look, we have Heidi here with us today." Because I have put Claire's hair in braids so the guck from surgery won't ruin her hair again (like last time). Claire wakes right up after the anesthesia and, not only can she feel her left side, she can move it. She is playing a game with her left hand. Praise God!

January 18, 2005

Another night in ICU HELL. But still, Claire is better and that retarded screaming child is gone (or was put somewhere else or who cares?) Claire is great, talking, moving her left side. They want to discharge her in two days. But I, who hate to make a fuss and want my child and I to be liked by her hospital team, say, "No! She will not be discharged this time until we know what is going on."

I want Claire to have in hospital OT, PT and all the stuff they need to do to make her whole. I am not taking half a child home from this hospital again.

So begins the insurance fight. Claire and I are moved to a regular floor. Andy Webb, (also from John's Creek church), shows up just as we are moving Claire from ICU. He says, "This is exciting, how can I help?" I say, 'Push this wagon, put these flowers in it'. We get into a nice room, off the main floor and Claire and I set up shop. She has her pink quilt, her pink pillow, all these pink flowers, the pink cat that Bobbie gave her the first time she was in ICU. It looks like "Pretty in Pink" x 4. But Claire is happy. We're out of ICU (I'm happy, too.)

January 21, 2005 - Margy

We get another CAT scan, and it shows that the cyst is shrinking. Praise God! The tech looks at Claire and says, "I know her, I read her web site." I think to myself that it's not much to read yet, but still it's nice to know that people follow her.

So, we wait for three days for Claire to be admitted to the Rehab unit, to get the help she needs to do the best she can with her life. Finally, today, Jim Kline, the head of rehab unit, comes in and says dramatically, "They have gotten the okay for Claire to go to rehab TODAY!" Hooray!!! We pack up our wagons (literally) and move up to the 4th floor.

January 24, 2005 - Claire

Being in this hospital is wearing on me. The food is horrible (the eggs made me sick this morning) There is no one to talk to here. They are all kind of brain damaged. It's hard to see people my age that wet themselves. It makes me realize how superficial I was and still am. This experience really makes actors and entertainers look small. I think our society should know more about how certain people have to live. Some of these kids may never have normal lives again. Their parents have some serious dedication. I mean they are giving up their entire lives to help their child. It makes me respect parents more. I see these kids and some can't say their names, the date, even "hi". Things I care about seem so minute. I want to just scream and leave and say "Everyone, back-off and let me go for a walk." But that would do nothing. I can't walk on my own, it's too dangerous. I realize I can't do anything on my own, except maybe cook.

Caring Bridge Entry:

Tuesday, January 25, 2005 6:43 PM CST

Claire is still in Scottish Rite. She will go home Friday. She is doing so much better in rehab. She has Pt, Ot, any T you can imagine. Her gait is almost back to normal and she is using her left hand for the first time in 3 months. I am teaching her to crochet. The best part is that her smile is almost back to normal, and she feels good about herself again. She is ready to tackle school and the world. Some of my friends from work came over last night, and the neatest thing was that Claire was back. She was talking to them and showing them all her photos. Please keep praying for us.

Alright, that's the positive spin on where we are. Here is the real spin. We are only in the rehab unit because I had to fight like the devil to get us here.

The good news about being in rehab is that Claire and I have hope again. She's doing the best she has done since October. All day long, she's in OT, PT, living skills, etc. In the evenings, Dave will come and take her to down to the cafeteria for dinner; it's good for him and Claire, and I enjoy my little break. It's the first time Claire has gone forward since she was diagnosed a year ago.

Yesterday, the rehab folks gave Claire a safety belt to put on her waist. It goes around her waist and whoever is walking with her, will hold it so she doesn't fall. The tech walked back to the room with the "belt" on Claire. I could tell by the look on my daughter's face that she was mad. The tech says that Claire has called the belt a "leash." She looks at me, like I'm supposed to deny that it is a leash. I don't know what to say; it IS a leash. However, I thoughtfully remain silent.

The tech says, "Well, it isn't a leash. We told Claire she can decorate it and make it look really pretty."

Claire says, "I can decorate it with diamonds or ribbons, and paint it pink, but it will still be a leash." Only Claire.

But she's doing so well. She walks, with a minimum of a list to the left side. Her strength is so much better. She's in all these classes, where she shines. And she gets to go to hospital school, where they're trying to catch her up. She is so happy with herself. Tomorrow I am going to work for eight hours. I'm looking forward to being a nurse again, for just a little while, and I know that Claire will be okay. Maybe we are finally taking a step forward.

Probably the saddest part about being here is seeing these other children. Children that were normal before their car wrecks. Claire says she was playing cards with one girl (who was beaten up in a home invasion on New Year's Eve) and Claire was winning, only the girl didn't know she was losing. Or, I was standing near our room and the techs were giving this one child (he's 16 years old) his weekly bath and he must have mumbled something about not liking to wear diapers. The nurse said, "If you don't want to wear diapers, don't poop in your pants." How sad!

The other night, I was in the basement of the hospital, doing the laundry. My sister, Cindy, called and said, "Guess where I am?" Since I'm watching the dryer spin, I said I couldn't guess. She said Paul, her husband, had gotten last minute invitations to one of the inaugural balls for George Bush from a friend at work.

Cindy was calling from the ball, telling me all about her formal dress and Paul's tuxedo and, as I stare at the grey cement walls in the laundry room, and listen to the dryer turning, I thought "So, who did I piss off?" Still, though, I was glad for my sister and Paul. "Take plenty of pictures," I said, "and have fun."

January 28, 2005 - Margy

We are home! I never knew HOME could feel so GOOD. To sleep in our own bed. To be free. Claire is doing so well, walking on her own. I'm thinking maybe she can make it to the last basketball game and wear her cheerleading uniform (although I haven't told her that yet, I don't want her to be too disappointed if it doesn't work out). Claire is walking alone, and can feel her left side again. It seems so much better. I think the surgery is a success!

Caring Bridge Entry:
Saturday, January 29, 2005 4:29 PM CST

Claire got home from the hospital yesterday, and we brought the ice storm on our heels. She was so excited to get home and so were the dogs. She unpacked all her gifts and added them to her room and then we just relaxed. Today we went down to Emory to pick up Hayley who was "iced in." The ice on the trees was pretty, like shimmering crystal.

Claire is back on chemo for 5 days, she goes on it each month, so she's a bit nauseated. But overall, doing a lot better. We were excited to hear that her new friend Will's MRI showed no tumor growth. Thank you all for your prayers and notes. Thank you, Nancy, (Will's mom) for telling us about Caring bridge.

I underestimated what I said about Claire. She is better, but so sick this time on chemo. Maybe that means that it's working. Still, though, she is walking on her own. Today she wanted to go out for a walk, so we took the walker and walked down the street. Who drives up, but Bertha and her daughter, Kendra, our neighbors. Kendra and Claire were in cheerleading together, and have known each other since they were in kindergarten. Bertha and Kendra wave to Claire, but you can see the disbelief in their eyes. I hope Claire doesn't see it.

Tonight was supposed to be Kelsey's birthday party, but they had to cancel it, due to the snow. But Fran said to come over anyway. I drive Claire, Hayley and Grant over there (one block away). Claire can't climb up their hill, so Mr. Tony and Dave (Courtney's husband) come out and carry Claire up the hill. She's so glad to be there and be part of the party. It helps, in times like these, to have friends who like us.

My mom and Uncle Gordy (her brother) have been sending money to help us out. What a Godsend! It's saved me a couple of times now. I honestly don't know what I would have done without the help of friends and family.

February 1, 2005 - Margy

Even with the money from my mom and Uncle Gordon, it's not enough. I need some steady money, since I can no longer work fulltime. So, I'm at my appointment in the Social Security office, trying to get extra money for Grant's disabilities. I don't know what else to do, I can't keep accepting charity from relatives and Grant is learning disabled, and maybe we can get some money for him. (One of the neighbors, who's son is less disabled than Grant, has suggested this idea, because she has gotten money from Social Security for years. Why didn't I know about this?)

I have left Claire at home alone, but she has her cell phone. Grant and I wait for two hours and finally are called back. We are at a window, waiting, when an incredibly deformed woman rolls up to us, in her wheelchair. Actually, she doesn't roll up, she blows into a tube-like device that makes her wheelchair move.

I don't think we're going to get a lot of sympathy from her. We go through all our forms and she takes a deep breath (probably more because she needs the oxygen than because of what she is about to say). She tells us that Grant is not eligible for help because Dave is still paying child support for him. Grant will be eligible when Dave stops paying child support in June 2005. I'm trying not to cry, but I am so upset and frustrated. Finally, I blurt out, "I don't know what else to do. I can't work full time because my daughter has a brain tumor and needs me at home, and Grant is learning disabled and can't get a job. I need some help somewhere." The woman with the breathing tube says, "YOU have a DAUGHTER with a BRAIN TUMOR? Why didn't YOU tell me? Why are you wasting your time trying to get help for HIM (twists her head at Grant, since she can't move her hands) when you have a child with a brain tumor?"

I whisper, "Yes, Claire has a brain tumor." The tube woman looks at me with new respect and says, "Bring in the paperwork from your doctor about your daughter and we'll get her into the Katie Beckett Fund, YOU will be okay." Great. So, whoever thought a brain tumor would beat out autism and a learning disability?!

Caring Bridge Entry:
Saturday, February 5, 2005 5:37 PM CST

This last week was tough. Claire was on chemo and the sickest I have ever seen her. Beside the nausea, she had vomiting, diarrhea and could hardly walk. Thank gosh for the walker!

But by Friday, she was better (had her beloved Mexican food) and I was able to persuade her to go back to her high school (no small feat. score one for Mom). She went half a day and had a wonderful time.

She's working so hard on regaining the strength she has lost. Her smile is almost back to normal and she's moving her left side more. Today, Claire and I went and had a massage at the spa—one of our Christmas presents from my family. Claire she said she felt the feeling rush back into her left arm for a few minutes. Afterward, she could move her index finger better. Guess what she'll be asking on her next birthday?

God, I should have been a lawyer. What a bunch of bullshit. This last week has been harder than hard. To see everything Claire has fought so hard for just fall by the wayside. She can hardly walk, she's throwing up. What the hell is going on? If the tumor isn't growing, then what is it? Sometimes I don't think she and I can stand much more of this.

On an up note, Linda's friend, Reinita, moved in last week. She just got a job in Atlanta, and needs a place to stay. We talked about it before she moved in. I told her how sick Claire was and that she might not make it, and Reinita was ok with it. So, I talked it over with the kids and told them how it would help us financially and it would be good to have another adult around. The hardest one to talk to about it was Claire. She listened to my story, and then she said, "Mom, that sounds good for all of us." She stopped and thought a moment and then said "But, where will Reinita sleep?" I couldn't answer her, because I was crying inside. Finally, Claire says, "Will she sleep in my room?" I say, "Yes, if that's okay with you." Claire thinks about it and says, "Well, I sleep with you anyway, so I guess it is okay." So, Reinita moves in, and I mean, Moves In. She packs more stuff in Claire's room than I thought was possible, but it's alright. My children instantly love her, and she is so good to Claire.

February 11, 2005 - Claire

I never realized how much I affect people until now. I have forced Mom to lose weight. She never wants to eat, or if she does, she never finishes a meal. Now, I can't tell her about how it bothers me, but it really does. It's her way of getting through it, I guess. I make Hayley withdraw and disappear. She only does it because she feels ignored, and maybe if she is totally ignored, no one will see her.

I am so sick of waiting. Waiting for someone to bring me a drink, waiting for myself to feel better. Waiting for people to go anywhere. Always being watched. The only place I am sort of alone is in the bathroom. I feel like a celebrity who doesn't want to be one. Everyone knows how I feel, what's going on in my body, how much I weigh, everything about me. It is kind of weird. I can't do anything secretly and I am a very secretive person, but this is hard. Every time I get better, I get worse. It's a neverending cycle. It really makes me want to give up. I'm convinced the rest of my life I'm going to be sick. I have no dreams, no hopes, nothing.

Caring Bridge Entry:
Friday, February 11, 2005 7:30 PM CST
This has been Claire's best week since she was diagnosed. She went to school for all 3 days! (yeah, I got to go to work!) She got a poem published in the school book and, best of all, she's finally walking alone. Granted, she's wobbly, but she's doing it. Her strength is returning to her left side, and

she continues to do her exercises religiously. Her face looks normal and she is starting to feel okay about herself again. She went to the movies with Kelsey, her best friend, tonight.

Her sweet 16th birthday is February 24, and we were at a loss as to what to do. But Mary Campbell from the Brain Tumor Foundation saved the day. She got someone to donate three hours in a limousine ride for Claire and her friends. Claire is SO excited. Afterwards, they will go to dinner at a Japanese restaurant. Thank you, Mary, and whoever donated it. You made a special child feel special.

February 13, 2005 - Claire

I have never really gotten used to the fact that it is '05.' I have lived with this thing for a year. Wow! Never thought I would say that! You know I realize why adults like to help me. It's because they like to feel needed. With their kids, who are almost grown up, they aren't needed. But, with me, I need someone there always. They are so nice because they know they are needed.

February 16, 2005 - Claire

I found out my tumor is growing. I don't know what to do. I'm so scared. This is what I have been afraid of since I got diagnosed.

February 17, 2005 - Margy

I am writing this for Claire. This is what she is verbally saying, "I am so scared because I might not have that much longer left. I wish there was a cure, there are so many more things I want to do in my life, like graduate, get married, have children. At least I get to see Hayley graduate.

Caring Bridge Entry:
Thursday, February 17, 2005 7:42 PM CST

Well, after the best week ever, we get the worst week yet. Claire started having difficulty with her balance on Sunday and Monday. Then Tuesday, she started throwing up and Wednesday I took her to the ED. That was the experience from Hell. We waited seven hours, to be told that Dr. Claire would call us with the results. By that point, any idiot knows the news is not good. Claire's tumor is back in full force, in several areas. She looks terrible, has been throwing up, is sleepy. We have talked about what the end will be like. She doesn't want to die, but she doesn't want to suffer anymore. And she has suffered. Claire has been such a brave fighter these past 13 months. And no one knows what the future holds. But if her fight is over, she will be going to a better place. A place where she can do her beloved cartwheels again and again. Pray for Hayley, Grant and I that we can help Claire through this. I really have the best kids in the whole world. Hayley is skipping her debate at Harvard this weekend to be with us. The four of us are truly blessed to have each other.

I'm still so mad about having to sit in that ED for hours to find out the worst. The least they could have done was tell us and let us go home. I mean, they weren't going to tell me ANYTHING until finally I said "It is 7:30 at night, we have been here since 10 am. I'm taking Claire home. She wants to go home. So then they said that Dr. Claire would call me. I stop at the grocery store on the way home and leave Claire in the car. I am in Kroger's when my cell phone rings. Guess who? It's Dr. Claire, and even though, in my heart of hearts, I know what she is going to say, I want her not to say it. So we chat a bit and she apologizes about not being to get over to see us. Then she asks me if Claire is with me and I say, no, she is in the car.

Then, she says, "Good, I didn't want to say this in front of her, but the tumor is growing again, a lot." I am pushing my little shopping cart around the store; talking on the phone and I feel my world stop. I even stop pushing the cart. Dr. Claire goes on to explain how we'll have to examine new treatment options, but …..it's not good. I want to cry; but I'm standing in the middle of Kroger, and you don't cry in Kroger. Plus, Claire is in the car waiting for me. So I finish the conversation and put my little phone away and pretend everything is normal. What is normal, anyway?

Caring Bridge Entry:
Saturday, February 19, 2005 10:23 PM CST

Claire is doing better. She is up and walking with assistance. We guess she had the flu this week. She is not back to where she was last week (i.e. walking by herself and using her left hand) but she is better than Tuesday thru Thursday.

She has decided that she wants to fight her cancer and so Dr. Claire is calling St. Jude's and my brother has connected us with Duke University and Dr. Friedman, who is a world renowned oncologist. He called me tonight (talk about tongue-tied, I felt like a teenager) and he referred me to the doctor who now does pediatric brain tumors in children.

I will call her on Monday. Meanwhile, Claire has her limo ride tomorrow with her dear friends and then dinner @ Hachi/Hachi, the Japanese place she loves. She is looking forward to this. Please Pray for her. She is so strong and such a fighter, and she needs to know that people are behind her. Her beloved French teacher, Madame Shirah, came over for dinner tonight. Her cousin, Donna Garcea, called her yesterday and that meant a lot. And then, Donna's mother, Betty, called tonight and that was special. Tonight, Claire's friend, Lisa, her friend came over and watched a movie with her. These little things mean so much to her. Yesterday, Kelsey (her best friend) came over and stayed with her. Claire is such a "people person," she really enjoys being around others and it keeps her from feeling sorry for herself.

Today, Nancy Olson called with new news about brain cancer treatments, and I will talk to the pediatric oncologist on Monday about that. And Dr. Claire has been so supportive. So many people love Claire and that means so much to her. Keep praying for us, we need it.

February 20, 2004 - Margy

Well, after making Hayley skip her debate trip last weekend (because I thought Claire was going to die) Claire is okay. So now, Hayley is mad at me. I want to say, "Well, I'm sorry I made you miss your debate trip and Claire didn't die." At least Hayley has a life. God, this is Hell. When does it end? At least Claire is a little better. She told me tonight that she is like my very own live Barbie doll, because I have to help dress her, and she and I have both always loved Barbie. How sad, but true. Wish it wasn't so.

I keep thinking she might die before her birthday. She always used to be so excited about her sweet sixteen birthday. Now, it's like she doesn't even care. Her limo ride is tomorrow and maybe that and being with friends will liven her up.

Caring Bridge Entry:
Sunday, February 20, 2005 10:13 PM CST

Today was a wonderful day for Claire. Even though she has a cold, and was a little nauseated, she had enough energy to get through it and enjoy it. She went to lunch with her dad and sister, Hayley. At 2:00, Trish, a friend from work, came over and gave her an IPOD for her birthday. She was SO excited. Then at 3:00 p.m., the limousine arrived to take she and her friends on her birthday ride around Atlanta. She had her friends, Kelsey, Lisa, Katie, Ashley, Ansley, sister Hayley; and my friend Lane and me. It was the neatest limo, with a lighted ceiling. The limo was supplied by Mary Campbell and the Brain Tumor Foundation, and they also paid for dinner at a Japanese steak house. Riding in the limo we saw Centennial Park, the governor's mansion and all the houses along Mount Paran. Debbie, our limo driver, has driven a lot of famous people around Atlanta and knew a lot of Atlanta history, so she was really a great commentator. It was a special day for Claire and I think she realized how much her friends love and are praying for her. She went to sleep with a smile on her face tonight, for the first time in a long while.

The Caringbridge site is the edited version of today. The real scoop is that I was afraid that Claire wasn't going to live to celebrate her birthday. She has been so nauseated and vomiting from the brain tumor, that she was on Phenergan and Zofran at the same time. Today, when we went to put on her pretty pink party dress (that we had bought eight months ago) it was all I could do not to cry. She had looked so pretty and healthy in it when we bought it. Today, she just looks like some bizarre caricature of Claire. Her face is swollen and her eyes are going in different directions and she can't stand alone. How can this be Claire? Did someone take my daughter and replace her with a changeling while I was asleep? Later, when she has me help her comb her hair, it is all dry and brittle. Claire's hair is never like that, it's always strong and shiny, even after radiation.

The highlight of the day was when Trish gives Claire the IPOD. Claire is so delighted with it; she has wanted one for awhile. What a kind gift to give her, and they don't even know her that well.

Then, there's the limo ride. I was terrified Claire would throw up all over it, but luckily, the meds held that off. It was wonderful, since none of us had ever been in a limo, but the ride was about an hour too long. Lane came and she got carsick. It was just so hard to look at Claire, amongst her normal, healthy girlfriends (who are having a great time, by the way) and she's doing her best to hold up her head and not vomit.

Dinner was good, but again, way too long. The service was so slow and the bathrooms were in another building (honest). For someone like Claire who has to go every twenty minutes, and can't walk, it was difficult. I just wish once someone else could take her to the bathroom. But they can't, because she's embarrassed and won't let them.

Overall, today was very nice, and people were so kind to do all they did. Claire did have a nice time, and so did the other kids, and that's what is important. And Hayley finally said tonight, "Mom, I'm glad I didn't go on the debate trip. It was important that I was there for you and Claire today. You did the right thing talking me out of it." That made me feel better, and I do need her here with me. I think she's the only half normal person left in this crazy family.

Caring Bridge Entry:
Monday, February 21, 2005 10:31 PM CST

Today was another great day for Claire. Her other best friends, Katie and Lisa, came over and spent the day with her. They watched an awful movie, "Mulan 2" then made cookies. Lisa and Katie helped Claire get dressed and took her on a walk in our neighborhood. Katie and Lisa are the people that keep Claire fighting. She had such a good time. The more Claire knows that people are praying for her, the better. Katie and Lisa got her home and after they left, Claire felt sad. But then, "24" was on and we enjoyed that. I spoke with Dr. Claire, my Claire's doctor. We're waiting until all the test results are in to decide what trial will be best for her. There are several options available and we will go from there. My daughter wants to fight this thing, and we are all behind her 100%. Please keep praying for our family.

Caring Bridge Entry:
Tuesday, February 22, 2005 10:49 PM CST

Claire felt good again today and we went to lunch at On the Border, one of her favorite restaurants. Then, her very good friend, Ana, and her mom, Jemma, came over. Claire's dad took her dinner and when they got back, her old friends, Sam and Ali, along with their mother, Tracy, came to see her. It really helps her to have all her friends around, supporting her. We'll talk with Dr. Claire later on this week about what the best treatment options are, and we'll decide from there. Meanwhile, Grant and Hayley are trying to cope with life w/o a car, since their car has died and needs a new transmission. Is life ever simple?

The real scoop: Dave called last week and said that since Claire's days are numbered, he would like to see more of her. I said sure. No one ever said he couldn't see her when her days weren't numbered. Tonight, he and I talk on the back porch. I have a list of requests. I tell him that since I can no longer work, I need him to give me an extra $500 a month until whatever is going to happen happens. I also tell him that I want him to give Grant and Hayley his ugly orange car when he gets a new one. They have to have some form of transportation.

Finally, I tell him that I want him to cover the funeral expenses out of Claire's college fund. And that he can keep the rest of the fund, or use it for Grant and Hayley. I also tell him that after Claire is gone, I want him to handle the funeral arrangements. Finally, I stop and Dave says he'll think about my requests and let me know. We sit there and look at each other for a long minute. What a sad thing for any couple, married or divorced, to have to do. To have to discuss the death of their child. There isn't anything sadder in the whole world.

The other scoop: The reason Grant and Hayley have no car is because Grant stupidly drove the car (that my mom got them) into a ditch while he was off-roading and destroyed the transmission. Will he ever grow up? I don't need his shenanigans at this point in my life.

Caring Bridge Entry:
Wednesday, February 23, 2005 4:40 PM CST

Claire had another nice day. She went to occupational therapy and physical therapy. She saw Dana, her physical therapist, whom she has bonded with. Claire's walk is better, and her speech is less slurred, but still slurred. She is more at peace. She talks a lot about the past, and her 8th grade trip with Kelsey, her best friend. And about going to Hilton Head last summer with Linda, Amelia, Keeley, Hayley, Grant and me; And the trip to Dominican Republic with her Dad and Hayley last June. She also likes to talk about our trip to Europe with my sister in September, and the cruise we all went on, right before she was diagnosed, 13 months ago.

We will meet with Dr. Claire on Friday to find out what treatment options are available. Claire is very excited because tomorrow is her 16th birthday and she will spend day at the spa getting a massage, a manicure and pedicure and makeup by her good friend, Olivia.

No matter what the future holds, Claire is ok right now. She knows that she is loved.

February 24, 2004 - Margy

Dave gets back to me and agrees to all of my requests. He will give me the money I need, and he will give Hayley and Grant his old car. (he has decided to buy himself a new car) Since he and I have been divorced, he has never agreed to anything I have requested, until now. Dave understands how bad this situation is, or he wouldn't be helping me. How sad for all of us!

Tonight, I am tucking Claire in, and I say "Claire, I LOVE you so much. I wish you didn't have to go through this." Because I do, so very much. It feels like my heart is tearing into two pieces to see her like this. She says the oddest thing to me as I hug her. She says, "I'll stay as long as I can." Does that mean she IS going to die? And that she knows it?

Caring Bridge Entry:
Thursday, February 24, 2005 10:37 PM CST

Happy Birthday Claire! When we came home from the spa, Beth, the nurse from Northview High School, had delivered a car full of flowers and presents. We are unable to see the top of our kitchen table; there are so many flowers and gifts. We went to dinner with Reinita at Longhorn Steakhouse. Then came home and Shelley, Fran, Tony, Kelsey, Jemma and Anna came over. It was like a party that went on all night. Claire had such a great time and felt so special. She got wonderful gifts, including a beautiful ring from Grandma, a pink watch and jewelry from Aunt Cindy and Uncle Paul, lotions and flowers from Uncle Chuck and on and on and on. Too much to list here.

Tomorrow we meet with Dr. Claire to decide treatment options and, prayerfully, we hope she will have the magic cure for Claire. Thank you each and everyone for your love, prayers and support.

After we got home from the restaurant, and she was in bed, Claire said she had an odd experience. She said she was feeling afraid of dying, a feeling she has had a lot lately. And then she said she heard God say, "Do not be afraid, for I am with you." And she said it made her feel better.

We are trying to decide treatment options. I have talked to everyone. One of the options is to take Claire to Washington, DC (where Cindy and Paul live) and stay with them while we try a very experimental option. I'll know more after I talk to Dr. Claire.

February 25, 2005 - Claire

Hayley found out yesterday that she made it into Georgia Tech. She's very excited. I found out today that my year of suffering will only continue. There is no a guarantee that I am going to live. Nobody saying "Life approved," you're going to be okay. This scares me. We are going up to Washington, D.C. for treatment. I don't know if I really had a choice in that, but I'm still overwhelmed. I had my 16th birthday, hopefully, not my last birthday!! I went to the spa. I got a manicure, a pedicure, and a massage. It was wonderful and I have already ruined it!!! LOL? It scares me to think everyone thinks I'm dying. It sort of makes me think I am, but I know I'm not. I mean I know I won't live to be as old as Mom, but I'm not going to die young. I seriously have no privacy. I mean everyone knows everything, all the time. I feel like a celebrity! I got so many presents for my birthday! It was like I was a princess. Mom got mad at me for being selfish on my birthday. If I can't be selfish then, when can I?

Quilt
Alone in my quilt
I cry in silence
No one to comfort me
No one knows
I think of my dreams
Along the boulevard of broken dreams
I think of my life
How I want something more
I think of how I might not make it to eighteen
This makes me cry
This scares me

February 25, 2005 - Margy

God, what a visit from hell seeing Dr. Claire is. I mean, it's not her, it's the news she is delivering. It's like I think it can't get much worse, but oops, it just did. Dr. Claire goes over our options with me, Dave, Grant and Claire. We sit in the world's tiniest office, all in a circle. Claire is across from me, in her cute little skirt and pretty blouse. She is turned toward Dr. Claire in such a way that I can only see her profile because her bright blond hair covers the rest. She is resting her chin on her right hand. And to look at her, right then and there, just like that, you would never know that there is ANYTHING wrong with her. She looks so normal and she is DYING of a brain tumor. She should be sitting like that in English class and thinking about her the next football game, or what boy she likes or what she's doing this weekend, or what she wants for her future. She should not have to be sitting here, in this little office listening to the fact that we can try these options, but there is no guarantee; oh, and if the worst happens, let me tell you what your death will be like...

February 26, 2005 - Claire

The hardest thing for me is not to be able to walk. In the mornings, I have to lay in bed, waiting for Mom to getup before I can do anything. I realize I don't have a normal teenage life. Most are worried about boyfriends and I'm worried about my life. We are going shopping with Fran and Kelsey, which means looking at what everyone else wants instead of what I want. Life is tough, or at least mine is.

Mom is the worst roommate ever. She is not organized and doesn't care. This bothers me a lot. I can't organize it, which bothers me. She doesn't want me to go to Camp Sunshine. She doesn't want to say it, though. She says it by offering other bribes. Erika and Laurie are here, even though I said not to come this weekend. I hate my life, everything about it. I'm so scared.

Caring Bridge Entry:
Sunday, February 27, 2005 2:08 PM CST

Friday was a tough day for us, as we listened to our options for the treatment. We have chosen to go with an experimental drug, Zarnestra, that is in Stage 2 testing. The best thing for Claire is that she doesn't have to lose her hair or get a permanent IV line. Claire felt much better this weekend. We're not sure if it's the rosary Reinita loaned her or the steroids, but we are all enjoying it. Claire got to spend some time with her cousins, Erica and Laurie, as well as Aunt Shay and Uncle Peter and her dad. She is looking forward to going to Camp Sunshine's overnight camp next weekend. Keep praying for us. We can feel your prayers.

Caring Bridge Entry:
Monday, February 28, 2005 10:52 PM CST

Claire is still doing well, though no one knows why. We went and exercised today at the forum and then went to our appointment with Dr. Claire. Dr. Claire has been so kind and spent so much time with me and Claire over this weekend, explaining all of our options. My Claire is going to do option #2, which is a trial study, and she won't lose her hair or have to have a port. We got all the tests for this done today, and we ran into our new friends, Nancy and Will, and got to spend time with them. We also met Will's sister, Claire. So, at one point, it was my Claire, Will's sister Claire, Dr. Claire and my middle name is Clara, we were all in the room together. We have to believe in Clairepower!

March 2, 2005 - Claire

I have been doing better, but I don't know how long this will last. I like know I don't really remember people, but they remember me. Mom is so mean in the morning. I mean I ask for one little thing and I'm scared to death. I'm afraid to move. Isn't it weird how I don't have any guy friends? None whatsoever. Yesterday, I went to the gym. I was exhausted by PT. I could do all the exercises. Oh well!

Caring Bridge Entry:
Wednesday, March 2, 2005 10:00 PM CST

Another couple of good days for Claire. Today we went down to Piedmont, where I work and the people have been so kind. Claire took two of her cheesecakes that she makes to share with them. Mitch, my favorite security guard, let us park in the ED parking lot. It was so much fun for Claire to see everyone. Afterwards, we went to the Mexican restaurant down the street, Casa Grande. The food was great. Claire continues to walk better and though her speech is slurred, you can understand her. She is okay where she is at. We will talk with Dr. Claire's office tomorrow about when she starts the experimental drugs.

Claire's Turtle Cheesecake

1 prepared chocolate pie crust

3 (8 oz) pkg cream cheese
1 ¼ cup sugar
4 large eggs
11/4 pkg semi sweet
sweet chocolate
1 (12oz) jar caramel topping

1 (8oz) sour cream
1 Tbsp vanilla
¼ cup butter
1 c. chopped pecans
1 1/2 cup sugar

Beat cream cheese at medium speed with an electric mixer until creamy. Gradually add 1 ½ cups sugar, beating well. Add eggs one at a time, beating as needed. Stir in sour cream and vanilla. Pour into chocolate pie crust. Bake at 325 degrees

For 65 minutes. Turn oven off. Partially open oven door. Leave cheesecake in oven for one hour. Remove and let cool, then refrigerate for about six hours.

Melt ¼ cup butter, and add chocolate morsels. Stir over low heat until chocolate melts, then pour it over the top of the pie. Heat caramel topping and pecans over stove. Bring to boil, stirring constantly, for two minutes over medium heat. Spread it over chocolate, cool completely. Is especially good if served with whip cream (Mr. Tony's favorite).

March 3, 2005 - Claire

I hate my medicines; they wake me up so early. Then I can't go back to sleep. Tomorrow I am going to Camp Sunshine. Something I never thought I would say. Wow. I do not like my life. Sometimes I think adults enjoy helping me because everyone needs a baby. And most of their children do not need them anymore. But I do. I need someone to go to the bathroom with me. I'm their baby because their baby doesn't need them. Mom is still incredibly mean in the mornings. It's not like I do this purposefully, just to piss her off. That is what she makes it seem like. Ginger is devoted to me. As I am writing this, she watches me walk down the stairs, waits for me, sleep with me, etc. I love her. I actually am jealous of Hayley. She acts like everything she has to do for me is a hassle. I mean, jeez, if I could do it myself, I would. I'm sorry my disease is getting in the way of her life. Dad wants to see us more. He thinks I am dying; I just know it.

I do not have much respect for the man. I mean, he's there during the decisions and things like that, but the rest of the time he's gone. He is too involved in his own life. Like when he got back from Florida and I was in the hospital. He went to watch football, rather than to visit his daughter in the hospital. I just feel like a big inconvenience to everyone. Yesterday we went to Mom's work; I can tell how much she misses everyone. It's killing her to stay home with me, although she says she wouldn't be anywhere else on earth. I don't believe her. I know she loves work and friends. I feel bad that she didn't even know she had a rash. She was so worried about me; she didn't notice she had a bad rash. I think I have more appointments tomorrow. Fun. Not! Every time I'm sitting there, I just tune out the world. I think my way of getting through all of this is obliviousness. First, when I found there was something in my head. I though it was a spot. I didn't realize exactly how serious radiation was. Also, brain surgery twice. The second time I was doing word puzzles the day of surgery.

<u>Need</u>
Like a baby
Needs
a mommy
So do I
Like a dog
Needs
an owner
So do I
Like a patient
Needs
a doctor
So do I
I need someone
to do
Everything

by Claire Nelson

Caring Bridge Entry:
Thursday, March 3, 2005 9:15 PM CST
Claire had ANOTHER great day today. She went to school for a couple of periods. We got there in time for French and when I wheeled her into the French class, one of the kids said "Bonjour, Claire." Then everyone looked up and saw her and

they all said in unison "Bonjour Claire!" Her French teacher, Madame Francisse, came up to me and asked me if I wanted to stay and I said, no I was just dropping her off and Madame said, then drop her off, we know how to take care of our Claire. She was so sweet. Then we saw Dr. Claire @ 4:30 p.m. and got the new experimental drugs. My Claire was nice to Dr. Claire for a change (Dr. Claire is wonderful, but my Claire can be less than polite to her sometimes). At one point, Claire's phone rang and Dr. Claire asked her if she wanted to answer it, but Claire said no, Dr. Claire was more important. Dr. Claire said, "Well, score one for me!" I'll score a lot more than that for Dr. Claire, because she has been with Claire all the way for the last 14 months.

Caring Bridge Entry:
Friday, March 4, 2005 6:09 PM CST

Today was another good day. We could getused to this! Fran, Kelsey's mother, my dear friend and witness of many miracles, prayed over Claire's new medicines last night. Claire started them today, with no side effects (yet). Donna, a doll friend of mine, came over and brought Claire a beautiful doll she had made for her and named "Claire." How appropriate. She will join Harriett's elf and Mickey's bear, all made with so much love.

Thank you everyone for the wonderful encouraging notes on the site. Thank you cousins Linda and Ted, for spreading the word among the other Claytons: it was so wonderful to hear from you'all. (Clayton is my maiden name) You are right about Claytons being tough, as I've often told my children. I know my dad, his brothers and Aunt Lucy are looking down on you proudly for supporting us.

I read all the notes to Claire and she was very touched. Afterwards, we got up and she said, "I do feel stronger." She walked a few steps alone and we went to exercise and did 20 minutes on the treadmill.

I dropped her off for her teen cancer camp this weekend. She was so funny; she got on the bus and said to me, "I don't know anyone." Then she turned to the girl behind her and said, "Hi, I'm Claire, what's your name?" and she was fine.

March 5, 2005 - Claire

Camp is lonely. I don't know anyone. I feel like an outsider, looking in. I don't feel well enough to be here. I feel like this disease is holding me back from being myself. I am scared of being alone. I am scared to socialize. When I was at school for a few hours, I stopped traffic. It was so kool. Like everyone just stopped.

Anyways, Camp Sunshine stinks, and I am ready to go home. No one knows me or talks to me. For that reason, I just want to come home. Home is where I'm safe. I didn't get the rule about no cellphones, I told Mom I couldn't call her. Her words were "Call me tomorrow." We played Trivial Pursuit last night and I knew all the answers. It was nice to be the know-it-all I never am. It's nice to be awake and not yelled at. Being here, I hate. It's like everything I have worked for is so minute. Like I have accomplished nothing. I just want to go home. No one wants to hang out, much less with a baby. I feel like I am missing out on the whole high school experience. I don't know anyone. I have tried. Nobody wants to talk to me.

<u>Alone</u>
I sit in a crowd of people
I am alone
No one notices me
No one cares
No need for fake kindness
No need for fake smiles
Everything I have/was
seems like nothing
They can do so much more
They have known each other for many years
I know no one

By Claire Nelson

This is the worst experience ever. I must have missed the memo to come to Camp Sunshine like 5 years ago. I am so afraid of dying. I don't know if my brain tumor is growing. No one can tell me if or why. Everyone here is so healthy and I'm not. I realize I don't depend on Dad for anything. Everything Hayley does for me seems like a hassle. I mean everything! She always asks me why I need to do this. I think I am a hassle to everyone. Mom isn't working, Hayley acts like everything is a hassle and Dad doesn't know what to do. I am scared.

March 6, 2005

I am incredibly scared. I am currently thinking my brain tumor is growing. I have worked so hard and it seems like nothing. I shouldn't have to go through this. I have my life, doctor's appt, school, doctor's appt, school. Never ending cycle. I really don't like Hayley and am just sick of everything. I just want it all to go away. I just can't do this, it's too much!!! I just want a break. I want to know if I'm going to be okay. I just wish someone knew something. I wish someone could tell me if I'm going to die. I am so afraid I will never make it to graduation. I can just imagine an empty chair and a diploma waiting for me.

Caring Bridge Entry:
Sunday, March 6, 2005 10:03 PM CST

Claire had a great time at Camp Sunshine, and was feeling so good that we (Grant, Claire and me) went down to the Southeastern Flower Show after she got back. We found a neat orchid for her to put in the pot she made at the camp.

Claire is doing well, took some steps by herself and walked with the walker. So far, she has no side effects from the new drug. Tomorrow, we will see Dr. Claire and hear what she thinks.

Claire's sister, Hayley, got back from debating for the last time tonight. She went 4 and 2. We are all so proud of her that she got into Georgia Tech. Hopefully UGA will be her next accomplishment.

I guess saying Claire had a "great time" at Camp Sunshine isn't really true. She actually had a pretty lousy time, but I don't think it was Camp Sunshine's fault. If I have one regret with this whole cancer nightmare, it's that we didn't join Camp Sunshine when Claire was first diagnosed. They are such a wonderful organization and they give families and children with cancer so much support. Claire went to Camp Sunshine thinking the other kids would see her as she "was", not as she is. And of course, because they didn't know her in the beginning, all they know is who she is now. However, the caregivers were very kind to Claire and she said Will Olson even danced a dance with her. It made her feel good.

Grant and I pick her up today and she is so happy to see me, and be back safe with me. This is not normal. A 16 year old should hate to be with her mother. She made a cute planter she is proud of and some other craft items. I say, "Well, let's do something fun, so you can get your mind off this weekend." So, we all go down to the garden show, which Grant is dying to see, but unable to go alone, because he has no car. I'm not at all sure this is Claire's idea of "fun." but it is better than sitting at home and feeling bad over something that's over. We actually end up having a good time (Grant and I more so than Claire) at the show and talk all the way home

Caring Bridge Entry:
Monday, March 7, 2005 10:18 PM CST

Claire had another good day. Her balance is worse, but that's frequently the case with chemo. We saw Laura, her occupational therapist @ 1:00, then Dana, her physical therapist @ 2:00. Dana is Claire's third cheerleader. I am her first, Dr. Claire, is her second, and Dana is the third. We're all so committed to her. We had an appointment with Dr. Claire @ 3:30, which we made and were out of there at 4:30 p.m. a new record for us. We ran into Nancy and Will, who always make the visit more fun. Claire was a little discouraged tonight, but she's excited about going to school tomorrow. So far, the new chemo hasn't made her sick and her blood counts are normal. Hopefully, it is killing her little tumor cells.

March 7, 2005 - Margy

What's going on the behind the scenes. I feel like there is our public persona (i.e. Caring Bridge) and the true persona (my diary). The truth is Claire and Hayley haven't been getting along too well. I'm not exactly sure why. Is it is too much for Hayley to bear, watching her beloved sister fail, or is Claire jealous of her (like she is of Kelsey) or is it normal sibling rivalry? Perhaps, it's all these things. Claire wrote Hayley a poem about how she was worried about her and, of course, Hayley took it the wrong way. I don't know what to do about this (to be frank, do I ever know what to do about anything anymore?) Maybe it will work itself out. I am leaving Hayley to take care of Claire for a few hours, so maybe they will work it out themselves.

And to be brutally frank, Claire isn't too happy with me, either. She has become so self absorbed, which I accept, and dependent, which I also accept, and I know she feels bad, which I accept. But sometimes, she is just SO demanding. Like today, I get her up, get her to the bathroom, sit her on the chair in my room, let her pick out her clothes. Put them on her. Give her the hairbrush to comb her hair and finally, I say, "I'm going to run downstairs and get breakfast started. Are you okay? Do you need anything else?" Claire shakes her head no. No sooner do I get downstairs, than she calls me back up for some piddly little thing that could have waited until I came to get her ten minutes later. I said something sarcastic about her needing to give me a little space.

Afterwards, I felt bad for saying that to her. She does so well, and tries so hard, and this is so much harder on her than on any of us. She just reminds me of a wounded little bird that no one can make feel better.

Of all things, Claire and Grant have gotten closer. I never would have predicted that, because they used to hate each other. But, he's home a lot (his hours were cut at the pizza place, and school is only part-time) and so they sit and watch T.V. together. I think it makes each of them feel less alone. Grant is so good about carrying Claire upstairs at night when she's too weak to walk.

Caring Bridge Entry:
Tuesday, March 8, 2005 6:34 PM CST
From Claire:
Thank you everyone for checking on me and leaving me messages, it means a lot to me. I know most of the time I wish this wasn't me, but I'm glad to have so many of you supporting and praying for me.

I went to school today for two periods, where I learned I am incredibly behind. However, the exciting part was when I stopped traffic in the halls because so many people came to say "Hi." It was very fun.

I went with my mom to her allergist appointment. Boy, was that nice not to be the patient! The most interesting part was when we were driving on the freeway and I thought my double vision had returned. This was because I saw two yellow school buses. When I told my mom that I thought I was seeing double, she said, no, I wasn't, there were two yellow school buses!! That made me feel good. Please keep praying and supporting me. I need all the prayers I can get.

Love, Claire

Caring Bridge Entry:
Wednesday, March 9, 2005 8:40 PM CST

Today was another great day for Claire. Claire's "other mother," Fran, came over and helped her get dressed for school. Fran also took her to school and Madame Francisse asked Fran if she was Claire's mother, and Claire said, "Yes, she is my other mother, and Uncle Tony is my other Dad." I was able to go to work and see the wonderful people at Piedmont ED who have helped me and Claire and so much. Plus, it was fun to be at work! Claire stayed at school for four periods, which is the longest in a month. Claire said she felt like royalty at school, when she sat in her wheelchair and smiled and waved at everyone. Her friends, Melissa and Kelsey, took her out to dinner at Longhorn's. Claire had a great time and came back full of energy. We are very blessed to have so many people that care so much for Claire and pray for us.

Grant, Claire's brother, who has been under a lot of stress at the pizza parlor, (it was recently sold) went with his dad to Colorado to go skiing. Hopefully, Grant will come back on Sunday less worried and more relaxed.

March 10, 1005 - Claire

Today I am getting my nails done. I am so excited. They look so bad. Yesterday I went to school for a bit. I felt like royalty. When I go down the hall and everyone waves and say "hi!" it's like I'm a celebrity without wanting to be one. Yesterday, Fran got me ready for school. She enjoys this, I can tell. She used to get Kelsey ready this way. I think this is why she enjoys it. We went to school and people asked her if she was my mom. I say "She is my other mother." Because she is my other family. Kelsey is my sister and Tony is my dad. It's nice to know I have them. It's all so nice to know if I go anywhere, Cindy and Paul are paying for us to go up to Washington, D.C. So sweet. Their hearts are in the right place. Jenny hasn't talked to me for a year, Chelsea too, only made fun of me and Shayna, who used to make fun of me. They left this card in my mailbox saying "We love you and hope you feel better." Now if that isn't fake kindness, that is just a lie. I might actually believe them if they had spoken to me. Mom gets mad at me for doing nothing this morning. I am writing in my journal and she goes "Can you just lay down and listen to that!" I'm listening to nothing because if I found my IPOD, I would be yelled at. I just have certain things that must be done my way. I hate to be yelled at for doing nothing. I cannot yell back. Hayley is really getting on my nerves. She never has time for me. I need alot of help. She is always too busy. A couple of nights ago I asked her to make peanut butter balls and she said "Can I do it tomorrow?" She proceeds to do nothing all night and the next day she is, of course, busy. Tonight, Katie is sleeping over. We don't have school tomorrow. And on Saturday, I'm going to the movies and Sunday is my Basketball Banquet. I am also going to church with Ashley. Think of that church as a cult. No crosses, the guy talks on a screen. This scares me a little. Melissa and Krissy took me out last night. The food was, of course scrumptious. It's nice to go out with them. All the single waiters stopped by to talk to us. Then, I go getting yelled at for doing nothing, making no noise, trying not to wake Mom up. Melissa wants me to go with her to the Coke Museum. Anything with Coke in the title, I like. Me and Ginger are really close. At night we lay, holding each other and paw to hand. She is my little protector. No one touches me without being severely barked at. She watches me walk down the stairs, she is always there. When I was holding my Rosary and I prayed. "God be with me." she put her head on me. At Camp Sunshine they put me with the retarded girl who didn't know much--that was not fun at all. For that reason I am not a fan.

Aunt like you
You Love us
Like we are your own
We need you
So many years of not knowing
I am glad we got to know you
You are so kind
You never stop giving
Without traveling with you
Our trips would not be

Phenomenal
We love it when you call from so far away
We need you
You need us

By Claire Nelson

March 11, 2005 - Claire

I have no school today, like I ever have school. Katie and Lisa slept over. I felt like a baby because I had to sleep with my mom. I didn't get to stay up at all. I know it was for a nicer Claire. But, still, it's like I am a little kid. I can't do anything by myself. I can't be alone at all. It is nice being with them. They are so normal. Yesterday, I got my nails, hair and makeup done. I felt special. Which, of course, I love. I haven't even spent my birthday money from Dad, which is exciting. I need some new makeup (it is a year old) if not more. My writing is better today. That's good. I have decided I will not let my brain tumor grow. I am waiting for Hayley to wake up. We are spending the day together, because I can't be alone. I have some nice new bruises. I had Lisa work on my IPOD. It has gone from 32 to 120 songs. Everyone says it's so easy. I'm not getting the easy part. I don't like these morning where I have to wait for people to wake up. I feel I could accomplish so much more if I could walk alone. Oh well. Something I have to go through! People ask me if it is (you know, the constant doctors appointments) annoying. I just say it is something I have to do. People walk up to me and talk to me like they know me. I do like this. I was in the doctor's office and this lady walked up and started to talk to me. I swear people check my webpage daily. Ginger is my little protector. It is cute how she loves me so. She barks at people that touch me. She and I sleep hand to paw.

<u>Hand and Foot</u>
There are people there at my hand and foot.
When I walk anywhere, I am never alone.
People there when I go to the bathroom.
People there when it's time for bed
I sigh and people ask "what's wrong?"
I'm no princess
I'm not royalty
I need the help

By Claire Nelson

Yesterday I went to international night. I love shocking people with how much I eat. I am so skinny, they don't get it. Madame Francisse is always surprised.

<u>You</u>
You have been
Through pain
You have been through sorrow
You know what this does to people
We stick together because most people haven't gone thru this
I need you more than you know
I love to know you will be there
If I fall
I know I can call you anytime
You understand my points

To Mommy, love Claire

Caring Bridge Entry:
Friday, March 11, 2005 7:47 PM CST

Claire has had a good few days. Her balance is still bad, but today she could chew on her right side. It seems like one thing goes up and another goes down. Yesterday Claire said, "You know I'm like an old lady. I hobble around, I talk slow, I eat slow and I go to bed early. Actually, Grandma walks better than me. You know, Grandma is a neat old lady, because she doesn't let bad things get her down (like Grandpa's death last summer). I guess it's okay to be an old lady."

Last night, two of Claire's best friends, Katie and Lisa, came over and spent the night. They had a wonderful time making the worst cookies I have ever tasted, and just generally giggling. Today she and Hayley went out with my credit card and had a great time. Can't wait to see that bill.

Well, the Claire/Hayley fight hit the fan. I left Hayley home all morning to take care of Claire so I could work. Hayley ignores Claire the whole time. (according to Claire). At 3:00pm, I walk into a cesspool of anger and not speaking. I ask, "What's going on?" Well, that's the wrong thing to say. They both lit into each other and start yelling. Once again, in my new life, I am at a loss for words (in my old life, I was never at a loss for words). Claire and Hayley continue arguing with each other and I remember my childrearing manuals about letting the children work out the problem by themselves until fists are raised. I'm pretty safe on that front, because Claire can't raise her fists, and I've never seen Hayley hit anyone.

They both continue screaming at each other until they physically wear themselves out and stop talking. Now it's my turn. I say "Well, it's okay to disagree and it sounds like both of you have some anger toward the other one (I should have been a therapist), but the important thing to remember is that you both love each other. You always have and you always will, and in the end, that's all that matters." I thought that sounded pretty good, until they both burst into tears.

After all the tears are dried, I talk Hayley into taking Claire out to Kohl's and give her my credit card. Hayley says (out of Claire's hearing), "Please come, too, I don't know how to handle the wheelchair alone." I tell her that she does and it's important that she and Claire have this time together.

When they come back, they are giggling together. They bought Easter socks for each of us. Later, Claire and I are lying on the bed, talking. Hayley walks in and Claire says, "Come and lay down next to us." Hayley starts to lie down next to me, like she did when they were younger, and each girl would lie on each side of me. Claire says, "Not over there, over here, next to me." And Hayley does, and she looks happy for the first time in a long time. That night, after Hayley has left, and we're in bed, I say, "I'm glad you and Hayley made up." Claire says, "Me too. She was really happy when I asked her to lay down next to me." And I smile in my heart.

<u>Hayley</u>
I have looked up to you
My whole life.
You are my sister, my friend
You are always there for me,
Even when times are tough.
We used to share a bedroom when we were
Younger,
Now we share our hopes and dreams.
When I found out I had a brain tumor,
You cried with me.
You were there for me.
You are my sister, my friend,

The one I love,
You are the one I have looked up to my whole life.
To my sister, Hayley,

Love always, Claire

March 12, 2005 - Claire

I hate sleeping with Mom. She yells at me in the morning. She acts like I do this on purpose. As if I like being like this. It hurts to think someone can think I like hurting myself. I don't like being yelled at in the morning. I hate mornings! Never can I do what I want! She just yelled at me for writing in my journal! I hate getting abused in the morning. I am trying my hardest to be quiet, but it never seems to be enough. Hayley and Mom said some of the requests I ask for are ridiculous. Things have to be done my way, always! They asked me why I do this? I have no control. There is nothing I can do myself! I can't even go the bathroom on my own. If that isn't uncontrollable, I don't know what is. Well, now I am lying on my back and freshly yelled at. I hate my life.

Today we are getting Hayley's senior pictures. We are excited to watch. She is getting her hair dyed before it. Tears in my eyes come as I wrote this. People treat me like I can't complain because everyone helps me so much. I have to be what everyone wants. I can't be just Claire. Hayley says it's not like she sees the real me, she sees a sick person who can't do anything for herself. I am here, just covered up. Why should I show myself? People might ask "why I'm like this?" Maybe I am just this way after cancer. I hate being blamed for things I do not do. Mom will probably wake up and say "What are you doing?" I hate that someone would think I would do this on purpose. I guess Hayley and I have made up. She still does blame me for this disease. It's not like I wished for this to happen.

Ginger is my little protector. She is like my other half. She won't let people touch me, if it's not anyone in the family. She is asleep on my journal, right now, as I write this. Lisa worked on my IPOD and now I have 120 songs, as opposed to 32 songs. I think I like Italian food a lot. Yesterday and the day before, I had pizza for dinner, for breakfast and lunch. I think I-talian, as Grandma says, is now my favorite food. LOL! I voted for lasagna for dinner. John and Bill are coming over for dinner. This means I can't go to the movies with Kelly. Oh well,

I hope this isn't a fake friends like Kimmy, Alla, Chelsea, and Shayna. They sent me this card saying, "We love you. We hope you get better!" Somehow I know that wasn't genuine. Shayna make fun of me for being blond, Chelsea made fun of me in cheerleading (guess who made football cheerleading and Chelsea didn't?) and Kimmy hasn't talked to me in a year. Somehow, I don't take that card purposely. This morning I was just trying to lean over and get some juice. I mean, I can't even do that without falling. My double vision is going away, I think. My eyes are adjusting to focusing with two eyes. It takes some getting used to, really. Well, hope Hayley doesn't look too slutty in her senior pictures. I haven't done anything all day. I have only sat here waiting. Waiting for people to do anything and everything. Why not feel bad for myself? I can't do anything. We are going up to Aunt Cindy and Uncle Paul's for spring break. Today has been a bad day, a bad weekend. This morning, I wake up. I am yelled at. I sit waiting to make my cheesecake, but we have a girl scout who's selling cookies who shows up. I wanted to walk on the treadmill at the gym, but no time for that. I wish I didn't have this life. Everyone knows everything about me. I am serious about this. If I go anywhere for something, it's a **big deal** if I'm there. We did go on a very short walk after me not doing anything all day. People finally notice I have been sitting all day. I just really hate sitting here doing nothing. Some people are coming over for dinner and that will be fun.

<u>Scare You Away</u>
To Lisa and Katie
I need you more than
You know.
I need you more than
You make me feel as "normal as I get
You are there when I need you
I love you for this reason.
I know there is nothing I can do
Which will scare you away.
I only wish we could go to the same school.
I know you have both been through a lot
You are both very strong.
I need to borrow some of that strength
I am lucky to have you both

By Claire Nelson

March 12, 2005 - Margy

I had thought that since Claire and Hayley made up, our appointment for senior pictures would go better today. No. First of all, I have put off getting Hayley's pictures for so long that I can't anymore, I'm out of time. And secondly, I stupidly chose Sears because it's cheaper. Cheaper, yes, longer wait times, yes. We were there for three hours and Hayley's sitting took twenty minutes. In the beginning it was fun. We helped Hayley with her makeup and hair and the photographer had her pose in cute poses. But as the time went on, and Claire watched her beautiful sister getting photographed, she became more and more depressed and slipped further and further into her wheelchair. She has become so self-absorbed lately. I mean, I know how tough it is for her, I'm there all the time. But to begrudge Hayley this one thing, when Hayley has had nothing in her senior year. It makes me a little disappointed in Claire.

March 13, 2005 - Claire

Today I went to the banquet. That was hard. Mom verbally abuses me. I know she would rather be somewhere else. She does no job of hiding it. I am very tired today, due to chemo. It's my third week. Today I was lying down and Mom yells at me for wanting to go to the bathroom. Mom yells that I should only yell at her to come upstairs once a day. I didn't even call her and she came on her own. She also yells at me for having clothes that are hard to put on. I don't like being yelled at. I can't yell back. It makes me cry every time she yells at me for things I can't help it. Like not being able to walk. I don't do this purposely. Maybe it would be easier if I wasn't here. Everyone gets annoyed with anything I ask for. I can't do anything for myself and I annoy people. I need to do something. All I do is sit. I am verbally abused for things I can't help. I just wish people would not get mad at me, and wish this wasn't my fate. I wish people would do something for themselves instead of me. At the banquet, I got an award. This morning...I forgot what I am saying. I don't want anything at all. I have no dreams, no hopes, no nothing.

March 14, 2005 - Claire

Today has gone better. I'm not being yelled at for things I can't control. I think my little talk helped. My vision, my balance, my speaking is getting all worse. My arm and hand and foot are numb.

<u>Scared</u>
(Transcribed by Mommy)
Like children on Halloween
Are terrified of what is to come,
I, too, am terrified of the unknown
Little children scream loudly
I scream quietly inside
What scares the little children are
haunted houses and monsters
What scares me the most are
Doctor's offices and MRI machines.
By Claire Nelson

This is it. My little bit of independence is gone----I can't wear jeans anymore. That was the one thing I had. Wow! I can't wear what I want. I am scared. I can't do anything for myself. I think my brain tumor is growing. I am so scared. We went to El Porton, the Mexican restaurant, for dinner and it was good.

Caring Bridge Entry:
Monday, March 14, 2005 10:11 PM CST

Claire had her basketball banquet on Sunday. She made basketball cheerleading this year, but was unable to participate due to her illness. However, she did dress out and go to the games and cheer for the Titans. The cheerleading staff at Northview gave Claire a beautiful Titan award, for her enthusiasm and interest. Claire said she was very touched by this, and the award sits proudly on her dresser where she can see it from her bed.

Claire had a rough day today. Her balance was so far off, she looked like a wet noodle when she stood up. She and I fell so many times trying to get her downstairs, I have as many bruises as she has (not really, but working on it). Dr. Claire (whose office we were in and out of in less than an hour!) said to wait and see, as my Claire has been like this before. But Claire was very depressed tonight. This is so hard for a teenager to have to go through (or anyone for that matter).

On an upnote: Grant got back from his ski trip with his dad, looking just like Indiana Jones with his new hat. Mark Kopel, Grant's scout leader and "other Dad" for many years came over Sunday. He told me he wanted to give us "food coupons" to help out. I thought, great, we have sunk so low we're on food stamps. It turned out it was gift cards to Kroger and Publix to help us with groceries. Thank you, Mark Kopel and Troop 2000 for supporting us and for helping me raise Grant over the years. You are all awesome people and you exemplify all that scouting stands for.

On a down note, my mom, also known as an old lady, or Grandma, (see previous entry) or the reason I started this web site (i.e. so she could stay updated about Claire every day) is in the hospital with pneumonia and not doing very well. Please pray for her as well as for Claire.

Tonight, Grant cornered me and started in his accusatory angry way. He says, "Mom, I can't stand to see Claire like this. It's KILLING me. And it's killing you, too. Mom, why don't we just let her go, just let her die?" He is in so much pain. I take a deep breath, and for once, words don't fail me. "And just how would you go about 'letting her go', Grant?" I pause and then go on, "I mean, she's not on life support, so we can't pull the plug. Do we just smother her or let her starve? And what justification do we have to do that? Because she is dying? Is that HER fault? Is it anybody's fault? She wants to fight this and I will fight with her as long as she wants. Because you know what, Grant, after this is all over, the worst thing that you can say to yourself is, "I wonder if I would have....or maybe we should have.....I never want to have to think that. I always want to know that we did everything we could for her." He stares at me for a long time, and finally says, "You're right, Mom." And he seems more peaceful.

Today I had to tell Claire that she can't wear her jeans anymore, until she is better. They lay on her hips and are so hard to try and snap together. It takes forever to do it. And she goes to the bathroom at least every three hours. The elastic pants are just so much easier to get on. She got tears in her eyes when I told her. I felt so bad, but I just don't have the time to button them ten times a day.

March 16, 2005 - Claire

Yesterday was a weird day. I got an MRI and had to wait for the results. The tumor isn't growing, which is good. Today I got like a 3 hour massage. Daddy is taking us out to lunch. The news of the MRI comforted me, but I am still scared to death.

Caring Bridge Entry:
Thursday, March 17, 2005 3:19 PM CST

Sorry I have not written in a few days, but besides our other problems, i.e. Claire's illness, Grandma's sick, Hayley and Grant don't have a car, our computer went on the blink. But thanks to Kaj, our neighbor and handyman, we are up and running again. One blessing at a time.

We have had an interesting couple of days. On Tuesday, Trish, a nurse and friend from work (Trish gave Claire the IPod for her birthday), brought her cousin Kelly over. Kelly is a hair stylist and she foiled and cut Claire's hair for free! It looks so nice, and she is so excited to have it shorter. Then, since Claire was more like a rag doll than a noodle on Tuesday, Dr. Claire arranged for her to have an outpatient MRI. The MRI showed that the tumor hadn't grown in a month (that's good) and that the area of the tumor that affects her balance looks like it is dying. (also good). We were so grateful to hear that news Grant, Hayley and I danced around the room while Claire watched from the bed.

On Wednesday, Claire was a little stronger and Trish arranged for Ellen, a masseuse to come over and give Claire and me a massage at home. (I'm beginning to think Trish must have wings, she has been such a godsend). So, Ellen arrived and gave Claire a wonderful, quiet, two hour massage. Then it was my turn. We had the shades drawn in the living room, that rain forest music on and candles. It was very peaceful UNTIL Grant arrived home with a friend of questionable repute. They sat in the den (the next room over) turned Comedy Central up full blast and proceeded to laugh like hyenas (I'm not kidding) while Fran sat in the kitchen with Claire and talked softly. Then Kaj came over and began working on putting tile in the upstairs bathroom. (Our rug in that bathroom is destroyed from the dogs, and Claire used the money she has saved for six months to have the rug replaced with tile). We heard the steady bang; bang of the hammer, over the phone ringing and the dogs barking. Ellen said, "Usually when I give a massage, it's a lot more peaceful than this. There is so much energy in this house." That's one way of putting it.

On the down side, my mom is not doing well. She has had another heart attack, is in congestive heart failure, and is in ICU. My brother, Chuck, sister, Cindy, and Uncle Gordon are with her now.

I just read Claire all the new journal entries and she said, "I appreciate all the messages and they touch my heart to know that so many people care and are praying for me." It was great to hear from you, Craig. You were my favorite boy cousin when we were kids (also closest in age). I remember many fun times playing with you at Grandma Clayton's house.

The real story: The masseuse came over to give us a massage and she was in the kitchen, talking to Kaj while I took Claire to bathroom. As she tried to get up from the toilet, I lost hold of her and she got wedged between the toilet and the bathroom cabinet. Here I am, trying to get Claire unstuck, when I hear this conversation in the kitchen. It was like one of those bad comedy shows. And I couldn't call them for help because Claire had her pants down. Finally, I get her unwedged and up. Claire's face looks so impassive because of the tumor, but I know that inside she is scared to death.

Kai has been working on our bathroom. Claire has saved up $400.00 that people have given her, so that Kaj can pull up the carpet and put down tile. Today, he was over working on the bathroom and he and I were in the garage. We were talking about Claire and he says, "Do you really think she will beat this?" I had to stop myself, because I was about to say, "Oh yes, it's just a matter of time." I try so hard to be positive, that when someone is really asking me to be honest (like Kaj was), I have to stop myself and think before I speak. After a long breath, I say, "No, I don't think she will." That is the hardest thing I have had to say.

Dr. Claire has been talking to me about getting home hospice in for Claire. I have told her NO. I want to take care of Claire myself.

Tonight, Dr. Claire is talking about when Claire becomes an angel. She says Claire will let me know where she is. She has all these parents who have told her stories of their children after they pass. Listening to her, I think I have crossed over into the twilight zone for a minute. Then, I realize this is what keeps Dr. Claire doing what she does. Knowing that these children she loses will become angels, and that they will live on. What a wonderful person she is. But, God, I hope she is wrong about Claire.

Caring Bridge Entry:
Friday, March 18, 2005 6:17 PM CST

Some more good news. My mother is doing better and is expected to recover! My brother and sister decided to divide and conquer, so Cindy is coming up here to help out, and Chuck is staying there with Mom. Hayley, who is visiting her boyfriend Mark in New Hampshire, is mad she won't be here when Aunt Cindy gets here. I'm sure she will get over it, since she is with Mark and his Mom.

We saw Dr. Claire who was so kind and patient with my Claire. My Claire is looking more like Raggedy Ann every day and her speech is more slurred. Dr. Claire showed us the scan and the area in question really does look like dead tissue. Further, she said the other area that had grown in February, has stopped growing. The only thing we can attribute this to are all the prayers, encouragement she has received and Reinita's rosary. Please keep praying; maybe we can have a miracle yet. Thank you, Cousin Linda, and your sorority sisters for all their cards and prayers and we enjoyed your newspaper we received today.

Claire has been writing poems about her feelings about her brain tumor for the last year. Recently, with Dr. Claire's encouragement, we decided to try to print them. Lisa, a nurse at Dr. Claire's office, wants to read them and see if she can set any of them to music. How neat!

Thank you, Belleville Methodist Church for your prayers and concerns. I have wonderful memories of Belleville and Aunt Ruby when I was a child.

Today, Dr. Claire gave Claire her last will and rights for us to fill out. What she wants done and not done if she is to die. Dr. Claire was very kind about it, and kept saying "You know, we hope this won't happen, but if it does..." It is so difficult for Claire to talk and us to understand her. Instead of speaking with Dr. Claire, Claire used her head or the "thumbs up" or "thumbs down" with her right hand.

At one point, I ask Dr. Claire is we can increase Claire's steroids, so some of these symptoms will go away. Dr. Claire looks at my Claire and Claire shakes her head "NO " and puts her thumb down. Dr. Claire says, "Are you sure you don't want the steroids increased?" Claire shakes her head with vigorously. Dr. Claire looks at me. My Claire knows what she wants.

We get home, and Claire is laying on my bed, I tell her we really need to fill out the form before Aunt Cindy gets here. I say, "So, if you die, do you want to be buried or cremated?" Claire shrugs her shoulders. Me: "How about cremated; is that better?" Claire "Okay". We go through each of the questions with me prompting her. She really doesn't care; she just doesn't want to die. She says, "Mom, do you think I'm going to die?" I say, "I don't know, do you want to talk about it?" Claire: "No." Me: "Well, if you are going to die, you are to be going to be in a better place than you are now." Claire has a tear on each cheek. I wish I could comfort her better.

Cindy arrives today and I say to her, "You know, Cindy, you were here to help me when Claire was born 16 years ago. I hope you aren't here now to help me let her die." She looks at me in horror. Still, if Claire has to go, I can't think of anyone other than Cindy to be with me.

March 19, 2005 - Claire

Today was Kelsey's Party. I'm not supposed to be like this. I'm supposed to be able to walk, to talk and go to the bathroom. I can't speak at all. I am very scared. I am screaming inside.

March 19, 2005 - Margy

Kelsey's long awaited Sweet sixteen party is tonight. Claire has been so calm. Today, I said to her, "I am so sorry that you have to go through this, and Claire says "It's just something that I have to go through." She is so wise and so old. I want to hug her and kiss her at the same time (which I do). At 6:00, we go to Kelsey's party at the Clubhouse. Everything is decorated so pretty, and Kelsey is very excited. Claire is in her wheelchair and Cindy and I roll her around the room. She is like, "It wasn't supposed to be like this" (because she thought after surgery in January that she would be dancing at Kelsey's party in March) "I want to leave, I don't want to be here." I am thinking that the longer she's here, the more she will see more friends arrive, and want to stay. We finish our tour of the party and I say, "Do you still want to stay or go?" thinking, that she will want to stay, but she says "I want to go home." So, we make apologies all around and load Claire back into Cindy's rent-a-van. I say, "Do you want to rent a movie at Blockbuster? " She says yes and off we go to Blockbuster. She keeps saying, "It wasn't supposed to be like this."

March 20, 2005 - Margy

Well, we were supposed to go to Linda's for Palm Sunday, but once again Claire is vomiting. I call and tell Linda that we can't come. So, Linda says they will bring the party to us. Dave is supposed to take Claire out to lunch, but I can barely get her to sit up alone. So I tell Claire that if she doesn't feel like going out, she and Dave can stay in the den alone and have a picnic lunch. Her response is, "NO, I am going OUT to lunch with Dad." Okay. So, Dave arrives and Claire can hardly move and he and I have to physically lift her from the wheelchair into his car. They drive off and I think "Good luck getting her out of that car." But he does, and she comes back from lunch more content. She lays on the sofa in the den when she gets home. Keeley, (Linda's daughter, and Claire's oldest friend after Rachel) comes over). Keeley hasn't seen Claire in months and Linda and I are worried about how Keeley will react. But Keeley is such a trooper. She acts like Claire is the Claire she knew and stands by her friend the whole evening. We all should have friends like that.

Claire and Aunt Cindy have been working on her poems. Claire has about fifty of them and they are putting them into the computer. Claire sits with Cindy for hours while they get them in just the way that Claire wants them. Cindy asks Claire several times if she wants to quit and do it tomorrow. Claire shakes her head. "Finish them tonight." She is having so much difficulty talking.

Kelsey and Fran come over and bring Claire food and balloons from Kelsey's party. After they leave, Reinita brings Claire a piece of the cake and Claire says, "Thank you!" Reinita says "For what?" And Claire says, "For everything."

At 11:00 pm, Claire and Cindy finish her poems and Grant carries Claire upstairs and lays her in my bed. As he leaves, Claire mumbles,

"Thank you." Grant smiles. I get ready for bed, get in and tell Claire, "I love you." I kiss her sweet cheek. She mouths the words "I love you, too." We go to sleep.

March 21, 2005 - Margy

During the night, Claire throws up several times, and I clean her up and change her pillow case. At about 10:00 the next morning, she throws up again and she chokes on some of her vomit. Her breathing becomes loud and noisy. I ask Claire if she wants to go to the hospital, and she nods, "Yes." I ask her again, just to be sure, and she nods again. Cindy has come, and Grant is home, so we all try to get Claire up. We can't get her up, and she has stopped responding, and her lips are starting to turn blue. I momentarily panic, I don't know what to do. I tell Cindy to call 911. The fire dept and paramedics arrive, and they can't get Claire up either. It takes five of them to strap her in a chair. They have to use a band around her head to keep her neck up.

They take her in an ambulance to Scottish Rite. I ride in the truck part of the ambulance, since I'm not allowed in the back. When we get there, the ER is very busy and we are put in the smallest room ever. Cindy and Grant have followed us and arrive. Why were we in the big room when it was just Claire and me, and now that it is more people, it is the world's smallest room? They do a Cat scan, and of course, it shows that the tumor is growing, causing increased pressure in her brain, and that's why she is in a coma. I call Dave and he says that he will be over after work. Hayley is on her way home from Mark's and I tell her to take the Marta train to Scottish Rite, instead of home.

The ED doctor tells me that they can do surgery to decrease the swelling in her brain. I say no, Claire has made her peace. Dr. Hudgens comes in and asks to speak to me alone. We look all over, and finally find a vacant room and he says, "I just have to make my pitch." I say, "Okay." He says that he can do surgery to relieve the swelling in her brain. I say, "Oh, so she can use her left side again?" He says, "Oh, no, nothing like that. But it will allow her to wake up." I say, "So she will wake up and be the way she was before she went into the coma?" He says, slowly, yes. I shake my head. "No, she wouldn't want to wake up like that again." In my mind's eye I can imagine her waking up after this surgery and the horror of realizing that she is still only half a person. Dr. Hudgen's nods slowly and says "To be perfectly honest, even if we do this surgery, it would only mean one day, one week, one month at the most. We are just delaying the inevitable." I nod. Then he says, "I still remember the first time I met her. She was so spunky in her cute little plaid skirt with her pigtails." His eyes mist over. I nod. I say, "I have just one question. If we had found out about the tumor sooner, would her chances of beating it have been better?" He thinks for a long minute and says "No, it just would have meant you would have known Dr. Claire and me a lot longer. But in the end, no, it wouldn't have changed the outcome." We stand up and I hug him. What a kind man he is, to be so honest with me. I appreciate it more than I can say at this moment.

I go back to Claire's room, where Cindy and Grant wait. I call Dave and tell him to meet us at the house, since I have decided to take Claire home to die. Dr. Claire comes and I sign all the forms. Cindy leaves to get the van. Grant, a nurse, and I try to lift Claire into the wheelchair. To call her a wet noodle is being kind. We can't get her body to stay in the wheelchair, she keeps falling out. Poor Cindy is waiting outside. As we try for the third time, it dawns on me that if we can't get Claire in the wheelchair, how will we get her out of the van, or into the house? It's like Dr. Claire said to us an hour before: sometimes the patient decides where and how they are going to die, in spite of our best efforts to the contrary. And I think Claire doesn't want to go home to die. I tell the nurse to call Dr. Claire and tell her that I want Claire admitted. She does this and Claire has a bed within the hour.

Reinita calls me. She can't get into the house. Someone locked the wrong lock and now she is locked out. I look up to God. What more can happen? I tell her to see if Sandy has a key. Of course, Sandy can't find her key, but she comes over and does find a window unlocked.

Meanwhile, Hayley arrives. How much is a sister supposed to take? She is so brave. I tell Hayley (who is tired) to go home with Grant. Cindy and I will spend the night with Claire in her room. I call Dave back, tell him of the change of plans and he is there in about twenty minutes. He looks as haunted as the rest of us. We all sit in the room, just staring.

It's around 10:30 and Dave goes home, with instructions to call him if it looks like the end is near.

Hayley calls when they get home around 8:00 pm. Fran and Kelsey have come to our house with a note Kelsey has written to Claire. The oxygen people arrive at the same time. Grant tells them to leave, we won't be needing any oxygen. At some level, Grant understands this is it, more than the rest of them. Fran tells Grant to give Kelsey's letter to Claire. Grant says "Don't you get it? She's not coming home." Fran and Kelsey start to leave, and Fran breaks down in the cul de sac. She is, after all, Claire's other mother.

Cindy and I stay with Claire. Not only is the room smaller than usual, but it is on the main hall, which is very loud. All the other times, we have been off to the side, where it's quieter.

Around 11:30p.m., there is a commotion in the hall and the nurse comes in and Shelley has arrived. My dear friend who HATES to drive anywhere, much less at night (and who has to work tomorrow) has come to show her support. I start to cry. I am so lucky to have people who love me so much. I really don't deserve it.

During the night, Claire's breathing is so loud. I lay next to her and listen to it, and Cindy lays on the daybed from Hell. Cindy and I talk, long into the night. I think "God, if you were ever going to perform a miracle on Claire, now is the time." I look at my still beautiful daughter, my daughter. And I want to cry. But I can't.

Maybe if I pray hard enough, or hope hard enough or whatever hard enough, she will make it. Who knows? Even though I am a nurse and have never seen a miracle, maybe my daughter will have one.

I keep hearing this strange buzzing or ringing, like machinery. It started when we got to Scottish Rite ED and it is continuing, even now, in the middle of the night. Are they still doing construction?

Caring Bridge Entry:
Tuesday, March 22, 2005 11:35 AM CST
From Margy and Hayley: Claire had to be taken to Scottish Rite yesterday because she was vomiting. The CT showed that the tumor is growing and she has aspiration pneumonia from the vomiting. She is not expected to recover. Claire is not in any pain, and is resting peacefully. My sister, Cindy (also with the middle name Clare) flew in on Friday to be with us. She has been an enormous help and stayed last night at the hospital with Claire and me. Dr. Claire has been with us

every step of the way. Our Claire could not have had a better, kinder, more compassionate doctor.

Claire is surrounded by me, Hayley, Grant, Dad and Aunt Cindy, the exact same people who were there when she was born 16 years ago. We have appreciated everyone's messages and thoughts and prayers. It has given us the strength and courage to go on.

Claire is going to be head cheerleader for God's team in Heaven. He will be very lucky to get her, as we have been so blessed to have her all these years. Just think of her doing the cartwheels that she loves in Heaven.

March 22, 2005

How do you wake up when you have never slept? But somehow we do, and the whole gang arrives around 10:00 a.m. We sit by her bedside. Dave, Grant, Hayley, Cindy, Fran and I. We tell stories about Claire to her. We talk to her. One time, I say, "Claire you're going to be a cheerleader in Heaven." She squeezes my hand slightly and her eyelids flutter and for a second we see her blue eyes. In the evening, some of her friends come, Lisa, Katie, Ashley, Ana, too many to name. Lisa is crying so hard that she gets Hayley's sweatshirt all wet and still Lisa continues to cry. Fran doesn't want Kelsey to see Claire like this, and I agree with her. I honestly think a part of Kelsey would die.

The day drags on. We are surviving on adrenalin. Waiting for the end. Dr. Claire comes with an (?) uplifting story. It's about a child with a brain tumor who went into a coma, but every couple of weeks, he would wake up, and play checkers and lapse back into the coma. Dave and I look at each other, dumbfounded. If ever there was any doubt that we were doing the right thing by letting Claire go, this story cinches it. To have Claire wake up every couple of weeks? I don't think so.

That odd buzzing continues in my ears. I comment on it several times, but no one else seems to hear it. It is getting a little bit irritating.

For the night, I ask Hayley to stay. I just can't be alone with Claire, while she is dying. We switch off sleeping with Claire. Hayley and I talk long into the night, while the sound of Claire's loud, raspy breathing is beside us. I am so lucky to have Hayley. She is such a wonderful person, and I feel so blessed that she has stayed with me through all of this. She loves her sister so much, and I can tell that this is killing her. They were always so close when they were little. As we lay there, talking, it reminds me of the girls and me laying on our cots on the cruise ship 14 months ago. It is just me and my girls, together again. Only now, one of us isn't really here.

Once again, as I lay next to Claire, I ask God to perform a miracle. Make her wake up like she did in February when she had been sick for a week and she woke up and said, "Let's go to IHOP today, because that's where we always go when we have bad news." Please God. Please don't take my baby.

March 23, 2005 - Margy

About 6:00 a.m., Claire's breathing becomes more labored, more chaotic. I think that the end may be near. I call Dave and then my sister. Then I get up and take a shower. Hayley is still sleeping. I come out of the shower, and daylight is coming through the window. It's a grey, overcast morning; as ugly a March day as you can get. And somehow, I know that today will be the day that Claire dies.

It's Cindy's birthday, and I almost wish Claire could wait until tomorrow to die, but I don't think that any of us can last like this much longer, her most of all.

The buzzing is still going on in my head, and I am beginning to wonder if maybe that is Claire. I have heard stories of people that heard odd noises when someone is dying as if the person in the coma is trying to communicate with them. But who knows? Not wanting to think I have gone totally over the edge. I ask if anyone else can hear this noise? No, no one does.

Dave, Grant and Cindy arrive around 8:00 and Fran around 10:00. Once again, we take up the vigil around Claire's bed. Dave is angry that there is so much noise in the hall. I think maybe we are being shown that while there is death, there is also life. But, who knows?

We talk to Claire again, and we sing, and tell her stories of her wonderful life. All of us do this. No child can ever have felt more loved than she is at this moment. Several times, Grant starts to lose it, and Dave takes him out of the room.

I hold Claire's right hand, the one she can still feel. I have held this hand since the day she was born. I have watched it grow and change. I am not letting her hand go; I will hold it until she passes over.

Around lunchtime, Jamie, our neighbor, comes and brings us a great lunch. Of all things, it is her birthday, today, too. What a crappy birthday for her and Cindy. Then, Beth, the school nurse that Claire has always loved, arrives. We are talking about Claire and Beth says, "You know what? Tomorrow we'll have everyone at school wear pink." We all say, "What a great idea." And it hits me. When we plan her memorial service, I'll tell everyone to wear pink, not black. Because I want to celebrate her life, not mourn her death.

Finally, around 2:00 p.m, Claire's breathing changes again. Up until now, she has looked like she was sleeping, other than the breathing. But now, she starts to struggle, and her breathing is more labored. I have the nurse give her some morphine.

Her respirations become further and further apart. Sometimes she stops for several seconds. But then she starts up again.

At 3:40 p.m. on March 23, 2005, as I am singing "Jesus Loves Me", sixteen year old Claire Emily Nelson takes her last breath on this earth. She is gone. While she is breathing, she is Claire, but when she stops, she just becomes someone who has passed away. It is almost as if we can see her soul leave her body. Grant puts a quarter on each eye, because he has read that it helps the body pass over. Dave gets upset about this and takes the quarters off Claire's eyes. We all just sit there waiting for what? Then, Fran says, "Oh my gosh! Claire died just as school is letting out." We all look at her like she has lost her mind and she says, "School lets out at 3:40 p.m. everyday. And, Claire died just as school was letting out."

Somehow, this seems right. Claire has always loved school and her friends so much. Claire is leaving this world just as her friends are leaving school.

March 23, 2005 10:00pm - Margy

Cindy, Hayley and I drove home from the hospital. What an odd trip home. For Claire not to be there. She has been with me pretty much all the time since she was diagnosed. I keep looking in the backseat, to see if she is sitting next to Hayley, like she always did.

Still, it is good to get out of that hospital. I don't think that I can ever go there again.

I get home and Dave arrives shortly afterwards with Grant. Dave and I go on to the sun porch to talk about funeral arrangements. Dave is destroyed, he loved her so much. I don't think that I have ever seen anyone look so sad. He looks like I feel.

I reach out and spontaneously hug Dave. I say, "She loved you so much. And she loved to go out to eat with you. You are her dad, and she loved you." I feel like it is Claire, talking in my ear, telling what to say to her dad. Dave hugs me back, and starts to sob.

As I hug this man; this man that I have loved, married, had children with, divorced and have now lost a child with; it is as if we are coming full circle. The hurt and anger that I used to feel toward him is gone. And in its place is just an incredible sadness for all that we had and all that we lost.

As evening approaches, the neighbors start coming over. Fran, Tony, Kelsey, Courtney, Dave, Jamie, Jim, Sandy, Tony, Laura, Kaj, Reinita, too many more to name. We all sit in the den and talk about our beloved Claire. And it is healing to be with friends who knew her and loved her. I feel peaceful and then that darn buzzing starts again. Now, I know that there is no construction going on in my neighborhood at 8:00 o'clock at night. I know that it is Claire, telling me that she is still there, and she loves me. And as I realize this, the buzzing stops.

Epilogue

Caring Bridge Entry:
Thursday, March 24, 2005 10:05 PM CST
What a day!. There are so many people that loved Claire that it is unbelievable. We have had so many visits from family and friends. Today we arranged her memorial service. It will be truly special, to see so many people in pink. We have wonderful pictures of Claire throughout her life and I know that wherever she is, she is excited about such a great pink party. Thank you, everyone for your notes and support. It has meant the world to Grant, Hayley and me. I hope that anyone who knew or loved Claire can come to the celebration of her life on Saturday.

At Claire's high school, Northview, they had a moment of silence in honor of her. Everyone was very touched. I hope that all the people in the school know how lucky they are to be there. Claire used to say to me, "Mom, I just want to go to school so bad. I wish that people who are in school could appreciate how lucky they are to just be able to go to school."

Caring Bridge Entry:
Friday, March 25, 2005 12:32 AM CST
The outpouring of love and prayers from everyone calling and putting messages on the Web site has been incredible. My family and friends and her dad's family are flying in from all over the United States. Our house smells like a florist shop thanks to the beautiful flowers, and looks like a restaurant with all the food everyone has brought. My beloved "other family" at Piedmont Hospital has brought enough food and accessories to fill the whole kitchen table twice.

Today, at Claire's high school, everyone wore pink. Hayley and I went to see it, and it was so neat to see the halls filled with pink. Even the guys were wearing pink shirts! I know Claire is up in Heaven cheering them on for wearing her pink.

Tomorrow, at her memorial service, everyone will also be wearing PINK. We are planning a celebration of her life that we know will make her proud. Afterward, my neighborhood,

Parson's Run, is providing pink punch and pink cookies. Who could ask for more?

5:00 p.m.: More wonderfulness. The management team at Piedmont ED, Bobby Wright, Kathy Flood and Cindy Murphy brought over even MORE food. We had to borrow the neighbor's refrigerator. Piedmont has been so supportive of Claire and me, they have given us anything and everything we needed.

The Parson's Run Charity Guild just brought over soda and wine for us. That was so thoughtful and saved us from going to the grocery store. I could not have made it through this without my wonderful neighbors. They continue to drop over with food, flowers or just to visit. Having everyone come around has made this time so much easier. Hayley, Grant and I all feel so loved.

My brother Chuck, sister Cindy, and her husband Paul, are here. My cousins, Gordy, Barb and Bob are all flying in for tomorrow, and Claire's godmother, Barbie Markos is here.

We will post pictures later tonight of the kids at Northview with their pink shirts. Tomorrow we'll also post pictures of the sea of pink at the service.

We are bringing Claire's beloved dog, Ginger, to the service. Ginger was Claire's best nurse. She laid on her when she slept and she rode around in the wheelchair with her. She even went to the bathroom with her! Ginger has been so depressed without Claire. We are hoping the service will cheer her up... or scare her to death, you never know with Ginger. Thank you TJ, for the beautiful poem and note you put on Web. TJ is a great nurse I work with at Piedmont and your thoughts comforted me.

Thank you, Nelsons for writing on the Web site, too. I know that it would make Claire feel better that both sides of her family are coming together to share memories and celebrate her life.

Unfortunately, my mom and Uncle Gordy and Aunty Lee will not be able to come. My Mother is in the hospital with congestive heart failure and not able to travel. Uncle Gordy and Aunty Lee are taking care of her. She wanted to come so much but we will keep her filled in on the events on the Web.

Caring Bridge Entry:
Sunday, March 27, 2005 3:09 PM CST

Imagine walking into a church and 950 plus people all dressed in PINK! So many people told Hayley they went "Pink Shopping" before the service. My friend, Geri, wore a pink boa that kept dropping feathers down the aisle. Merline wore a bright pink hat. Maxine had sparkles all over and bright pink shoes. And Joella made it sans her Diana Ross wig. What a wonderful celebration of Claire's life.

The service was beautiful and Dee spoke eloquently. Kelsey's letter showed Claire as a teenager. Her dad's letter, and mine and Hayley's showed the Claire we had always known and loved. Her friend Melissa spoke and Grant finished up with a fitting tribute to his sister. I think everyone came to love and know the Claire we had. She was such an extraordinary young lady.

The flowers at home and church were INCREDIBLE! I have never seen such beautiful flowers. Piedmont sent a three foot megaphone of silver flowers and decorated in the school colors. We got several arrangements of lovely pink roses. My doll club sent a lovely dish garden, my book club sent a gorgeous arrangement. And there were so many neat plants, azaleas, lupines, peace lillies. Grant is so excited to plant the plants in his backyard by his pond. If I forgot to mention any of the arrangements, please forgive me, it is all so overwhelming.

Ginger, the dog, did very well. She was carried down the aisle by me, and sat in the first row with her family. When the music started, we thought she was going to lose it, but she kept it together and started looking around the church for friends. She stayed afterward at the reception until she started shaking uncontrollably, even her ears were shaking. She was escorted home where she was thrilled when we got there.

The reception was sponsored by the Parson's Run Neighborhood (where we live). And everything was of course, pink. Pink punch, pink cookies, pink tablecloths, plates, forks etc. Then back at the house, they had even more pink and food. With beautiful pink roses in the center of the table. The neighborhood took care of everything, including some well needed wine.

About 60 Piedmont people came and for a minute I thought we were back at work, only we were wearing pink instead of blue scrubs. I truly could not have made it thru this w/o the people at work. Kathy and Kristina covered my shifts. And everyone in ED donated time so that I could stay home with Claire. Piedmont is more than just another family, they took care of me while I took care of my daughter.

Dr. Claire came to Claire's service. It was so good to see her; I will miss her terribly. Although, I won't miss those long office visits. And Nancy Olson, my other cancer mom, who has meant so much to me was there.

To see all of our friends and family at the reception was so heartwarming. People came from all walks of our lives. My doll mother, Martha, and the other doll club members, my book club members, my neighbors, my old neighbors, (like Norma, my first friend in GA, and to her daughter, Rachel, who was Claire's first friend when Rachel was eight months old and Claire was four months old) , Then there were Claire's friends from cheerleading, her old boyfriend, Bryan, her friends from Brownies and Girl Scouts; kids who used to take classes that Hayley, Claire and I taught, Hayley and Grants' friends, my family, and Dave's family. It meant so much to see yall'.

We had pictures celebrating Claire's life on two tables in the chapel. Those two tables were more crowded than the food tables. It was almost impossible to get up there to see the pictures, because everyone wanted to get a look.

It was fun to share Claire as she was with everyone. Those pictures will keep her alive in our hearts.

I'll write more as I think of it. And, if I forgot to mention anyone, please forgive me.

What an unbelievable tribute to Claire's life! I will write more later, but now, know how much all of you have touched our hearts and souls.

Four years later.....

August 16, 2008-Margy

Four years ago, the lives of my family changed forever. From the moment we heard those words "Claire has a brain tumor…" nothing was ever the same again. So now, four years later, I look back.

The first year after Claire was gone seems like a blur of pain, more pain and oh yes, pain. So much sadness, so much remembering. For her first unbirthday, February 24, 2006, we had a Remembrance Party" for her at my house. I was worried how it would turn out, but it turned out wonderfully. My sister flew in from Washington, DC; we had Mexican food (Claire's favorite) and it was so wonderful to be with all the people that had loved Claire, and helped me care for her. It was like Claire was really at that party, in the spirit of all the people that loved her. We got out all the photo albums, scrapbooks and picture books of her life and we looked at them. And then we let 17 pink balloons go off into Heaven. As the balloons went up, they formed a "C" shape. I know what angel designed that!!

Our lives have gone on, as they do, whether you want them to or not. Some good days, some bad days.

Grant is doing GREAT! Words I thought I would never be able to say when he was growing up. Grant worked as a surveyor for several years and is now going to college at Savannah College of Art and Design, in Savannah. Dave used Claire's college fund for Grant's first year. I think Dave did exactly what Claire would have wanted done with the money. Grant wants to get a bachelor of fine arts from SCAD so that he can design homes, something he has always wanted to do.

Grant has had several girlfriends. His first one was Kristina, who had red hair like him. Since then, he's had several others. Grant is as determined as he's always been, and I feel like he'll be successful in college and life.

Hayley graduated from high school in May, 2005. Unfortunately, Claire wasn't there in person, but at the graduation and the party afterwards, there was always a seat on one side of me that was vacant. This was never planned, it just happened; so I felt Claire there.

Grandma, who wanted so much to come to Claire's memorial service, but was too ill; was well enough to come to Hayley's graduation. She flew up from Florida alone and was so excited to see her granddaughter graduate. At the party afterwards, she just sat, with the sweetest smile on her face, enjoying seeing everyone, and being with her family.

Grandma died peacefully in August, 2005. I know that she was met at the pearly gates by my Dad, my Grandma Clara and my Claire. Grandma was my family's third death in a year and a half, and the end of that era (thank God).

Since my mother has been gone, I have grown closer to my Uncle Gordon and Aunty Lee (my mother's brother and his wife). They have been like surrogate parents to me and have helped me cope with the loss of both my parents and child.

Aunt Cindy, after trying to get pregnant for several years, had a little girl in October, 2007 and her name is "Elizabeth Claire".

Hayley is in her last year of college at the University of Georgia in Athens, GA. She graduates in May with a degree in Statistics. She is still rooming with Maggie, her high school friend.

Though I wanted Hayley to be a doctor, she likes math and got an A in Calculus 3. I guess she's made the right decision for herself. She has been such a great daughter and best friend to me. I feel very lucky and blessed.

Funny, Hayley was always so quiet growing up. Since Claire has been gone, Hayley has become a lot more outgoing and silly. Sometimes she reminds me of Claire in the nicest of ways. She and I have gone from being mother and daughter, to best friends. I am so lucky to have her. Whenever she calls me, (which is frequently, thank God) I think, "Thank you God for leaving me Hayley." What a silly thing to think, and yet I am so glad that Hayley and I have been there for each other.

A few months ago, Hayley said "Mom, do you mind if I write on Claire's web site? I have something so say." So she did.

CaringBridge Web Site: Septermber 6, 2007
From Hayley:
At night I lie awake wondering what would have become of my Claire. I don't think about Claire that much, or talk about her that much. That sounds like a bad thing, but sometimes there just aren't words to express what I want to say. So I just don't say anything at all. So until they develop a word for

beyond sadness, beyond heartbreak, I will keep my mouth shut and not even try to express what I feel.

But, the truth of the matter is that is that I do miss Claire. She was an incredible person with an amazing zest for life that never went away. Frequently, I ignore the fact that I had a sister with cancer. It is just easier for me to deal with it that way, than acknowledge that I lost one of the few people in the world that I really cared about. So I'll go days on end without thinking about her, and think nothing of it. But when I least expect it, I see Claire. I don't see her that much, when I do see her, I know that she's there.

I look back on the wonderful times we had together and it breaks my heart to know that we don't have those anymore. But I do know we were lucky to have those times in the first place. Every time I look around my room, I see pictures of her and me, my favorite being the one of us in the Bahamas that she bought a special frame to put the picture in. I also see a wooden dog that I wanted so badly when we went on vacation, but didn't want to buy it for myself. Claire went back the next day and bought that dog for me, and it means the world to me.

I want to say that I think about Claire everyday and my loss. But, the truth is that I don't. But if it's easier for me to deal with it that way, I know Claire is not forgotten and will never be. I don't believe there is a wrong way to deal with grief. I don't cry about Claire, and I can't remember the last time that I did. For me, the experience was something that happened to me. I dealt with it and it changed me forever. But does that require that I need to sit in bed and cry about what has handed me? Is that what she would have wanted me to do?

I do wonder about Claire, though. I know she would have wanted to come to Georgia with me. That's just the kind of sister was (most say that imitations flattering, with her, I never thought that, but now I do). I'll never find out what kind of person she would be today. But in my heart, I know that she would have been a good, caring person. I do feel her presence though, and more than anything, I want to be the person she would've wanted me to be. I want her to look down on me and proudly say "that's my sister!"

It breaks my heart to know that I no longer have a sister, nor that sisterly bond that we shared. I do feel that someday I will find a person who is like a sister to me, not a replacement, a "helper". There is a lot of talk about parents who lose children (or so my Mom tells me), but I so rarely hear about siblings who lost their siblings. It's an untouched domain, that should be dealt with. It's an absolutely horrific thing to lose a sibling, especially one like Claire' and there is bond that absolutely can't be replaced. Some of the things that we said and did together are forever between us, never to be revisited because she isn't here to relive those memories with me. There is an eternal connection between siblings because you lived through so many of the same experiences, and when one of you is gone, those memories most likely die.

Claire was pretty much my favorite person in the world until she got sick. I absolutely hated Claire when she was sick. I'm not afraid to admit it, she wasn't very nice to me. How could she be, when she was painfully dying? I hated the attention she got, the gifts she got, that she got to miss so many days of school and the list goes on.

Claire was no angel, and I'm sure she wouldn't have wanted to be remembered as such. I know the person that I saw when Claire was sick, was not Claire. It was a shell of a broken person who used to be Claire and was trying to deal with the worst possible situation. Since Claire died, I've regretted some of things that I said and did to her, as well as more of things I didn't do. I'll even go so far as to say that I was mad at Claire, after she died. How could she treat me like that? And then die? It has taken me two years to come to terms with the fact that that wasn't the Claire I knew and loved. Every once in a while she would peak her head out, but mainly it was angry, hurt, little girl. So Claire, I'm sorry for whatever I said to you or did to you, and I forgive you for whatever you said and did to me. I know we'll meet again someday and be able to hug over this apology, but I really do love you more than you could ever understand. Thanks for being the best sister I could've asked for

A few good things have come out of all of this; Mom and I closer than ever. Who knew your family could be so cool? I'm thankful for every day that I spend with my Mom or even just talk to her. She's such a fun, neat, caring person and I don't know that I would've seen that as quickly had we not gotten the opportunity to spend so much time together. So, thanks, Claire, for bringing us together, even if it was in your absence. I also shouldn't spend time thinking about what could have been or what should have been. It's pretty irrelevant to the here and now, not to say that we shouldn't be sad, but that sadness is a never-ending cycle and isn't going to bring back your lost loves. I guess probably the last thing I learned was that we shouldn't take anything for granted. Enjoy whatever time you have with whoever you're with, and just be thankful that you're here, hopefully healthy and happy.

I love you Claire, I always have, and I always will and thanks for 16 great years together. I wish it was more, but I'm glad we had what we had and you will never be forgotten.

Hayley

One final thought: sometimes I think my Mom is totally crazy (in a good way) when she talks about Claire "visiting" her. But a few days ago, I work up from a nap in which I was helping Claire with her math homework. And I remember thinking as I woke up, I wish I could go back to that dream. More than anything, I want to go back to that dream.

Patti Phillips, my first cancer mother/friend in this journey, lost her daughter, Stephanie in January, 2005. Nancy Olson, my second friend (Will's Mom) and I remain close and her daughter, Claire, ran in "Cure" in honor of my Claire in March, 2008. Nancy's son Will, who had a medulloblastoma and stem cell transplant; is in his third year of college at Auburn University in Alabama. Though the chemo and radiation have affected his balance and hearing, he is doing well, his cancer has never reoccurred and it gives me hope for all children battling cancer.

Ginger Bridget, the dog, is still around, and as puppy-like as ever. The first month after Claire left, Ginger spent under Claire's bed. We couldn't get her out of there. I have never seen a dog look so sad. There is now scientific evidence that dogs can smell cancer. That's why Ginger slept wrapped around Claire's head and was such a good nurse to her. Ginger knew about the cancer before we did, and was taking care of Claire in the only way she knew how, by loving her.

After a while, Ginger did become my dog again, and once more, sleeps with and worships me. She now happily lives with me and our other dogs, Tinkerbell and Carter.

Still, sometimes I'll see she or Carter looking at the bed where Claire slept, and if I ask them where Claire is, they'll look to the bed. I know that if Claire would walk in tomorrow, Ginger would remember her and dash up to her and kiss her all over her face.

We had Claire cremated and her ashes are in a box with dolls on the outside of it, and the box is on my fireplace in the den. It gives me great pleasure when Hayley, Grant and I (and the dogs) are sitting in the den talking, and I look over at the box and know that Claire is here with us, too.

Kelsey, Claire's best friend, has grown up to be a beautiful young woman, inside and out. Kelsey doesn't remind me of Claire now, probably because she is older than Claire was when she died. Kelsey has a boyfriend named, of all things, Nelson. Kelsey believes that Claire sent Nelson to her. It wouldn't surprise me. I still get together with Fran and Mr. Tony and every once in while, a new Claire story will come out, and it touches my heart.

And me. I got through the first year of losing Claire just barely. If not for the love and support of my family, and friends, I honestly think I would have given up.

But now, four years later, I slowly find my love of life returning. I have started sculpting my babies and animals again, and going to doll shows. I enjoy my work as an ED nurse, and have been promoted to Clinical Manager of the Emergency Department. This job allows me to evoke change on a larger level. It is a challenging, wonderful job where I get to help staff, patients and physicians, all at the same time. I feel very blessed to have been given a career opportunity like this. I have an active social life, with many friends, and for the most part, I am content with my life.

One of the things that helped me to heal was meeting other parents who have lost their children. My first friends were Theresa and Jeff, (their daughter, Jordan, died in November 2005). They found me through Claire's Web site, and we met at a Camp Sunshine's grief group. They were the start of other mothers and friends that I have met along this journey.

We all belong to the club that no parent would ever want to join, and we pray daily for no new members. I frequently get together with Theresa and several of the mothers who have lost their children and we share our lives and feelings. .It's so healing to be with them; either in a group or just one on one. The best part is we can tell each other stories of our lost children. It's like, when we hear these stories, we come to know each other's children (whether we did in life or not) and our children aren't totally gone from us.

Another thing that has been helpful has been to edit Claire's diaries. To read the way she described her life, and to hear her wonderful voice again--to relive our life, has been healing. From the moment Claire was diagnosed, all my good memories of my children and our life together flew out the window. And after Claire was gone, all I could focus on was her loss. But now, with her diaries and mine, I can remember that we did have a good life, we did love each other, we did have extraordinarily bad luck, but we got through it.

And we continue to get through it. Some days, the pain of her loss is still disabling. But with enough distance, I am able to save that sadness for an appropriate time. Other times, seeing a little girl with Claire's blond hair and curls, seeing a teenager with Claire's face shape, or the way she walked can bring tears to my eyes. And yet, with time, I have learned to see that childs resemblance to Claire, and smile at my memories of her. Because while life can take our loved ones away; it can't take our memories. And I will always treasure my memories of Claire.

Finally, I have had many "visits" from Claire. Not the kind of "visits" where I see her, but the kind of visits where I dream of her, or I find things she left in the most unpredictable places; or I hear songs that she loved playing on the radio. It usually happens at times when I need to feel Claire around me the most. It let's me know that she is still here, just behind a curtain I can't open.

After she was first gone, I had a dream that I opened the front door and there was Claire, dressed in her pretty pink coat. She had come back to life to see me. But then, as she walked into the house, I saw that she was still sick and still couldn't use her left side. I said, "Claire, I don't want you back sick, I want you back the way you were before you got sick." Claire said, "But Mom, this is the way I left this earth and this is the way I have to come back if I do. So please let me go back so that I can fly with the angels." And in my dream, I kissed her sweet cheek and let her go back to the angels.

My most powerful dream was about six months ago. When Claire was alive, she would call me at work all the time and say "Mommy, guess what happened with Kelsey today? " Or "Could Cameron, Kristen, Keeley and I go ….." She was always so excited to do something with her friends, and she had so many friends whose names started with "K". Hayley, Grant and I used to tease her about how many "K" friends she had.

In my dream, Claire called me and said, "Mommy, guess what? Me, Jordan, Jarrett and Jennifer are having so much fun doing all this new stuff!" And, in my dream I said "Claire, who are all these 'J' people? What happened to your 'K' friends?" Claire said: "These are my new friends, and I wanted to tell you about them." And, in the dream, like a bomb, it hit me: Claire was dead, but she was calling me. I said, "Claire, is that you? Are you calling me from Heaven?" She said, "I'm not supposed to say. I just missed you and wanted to talk to you and tell you about my new friends and what we are doing." I said, "Claire, I know that it's you. Please talk to Hayley and tell her it's you, because she thinks I'm crazy when I tell her these stories about my dreams." I put the phone to Hayley's ear, but Claire wouldn't talk to her. So I took the phone back and said, "But Claire, it is you isn't it?" Claire once again said, "I can't say, I love you, Bye."

I woke up knowing that Claire had really called and I began to think Jordan….. Jarrett…Jennifer. Slowly I realized that Jordan is Theresa and Jeff's daughter. I think of Jordan as Claire's first friend in Heaven. Jarrett's mother; Michelle was my second friend I met who had lost a child. She and I think of Jarrett and Claire as boyfriend and girlfriend in Heaven.

Finally, Jennifer's parents have recently moved into my neighborhood. Jennifer died suddenly in December, 2004.

I had never realized that all these friends had children's names that started with a 'J'.

Having that dream lets me know that even though our children aren't with us in the flesh, they are still with us in spirit. They may be gone physically from this earth, but they continue to love us and think of us. And, if we look for them, and are very lucky, we will see glimpses of them in this life; and look forward to being with them in the next life.

Ginger + me on the first day of school.

August 2004

♡ ya Claire

To visit Claire's web bridge site, please go to www.caringbridge.org/ga/claire

Printed in the United States
136190LV00004B/2/P